Siud an t-Eilean
There Goes the Island

Sgoil Ghaidhlig Ghlaschu
147 Berkeley Street
Glasgow
G3 7HP
0141 276 8500

Edited by Ian Stephen

The publishers acknowledge financial assistance from the Gaelic Books Council towards the publication of this anthology.

Cover photograph: John Mackinnon

Published in Scotland in 1993 by Acair Ltd, 7 James Street, Stornoway, Isle of Lewis.

Designed and typeset by Acair Ltd, 7 James Street, Stornoway, Isle of Lewis.

Printed by Highland Printers, 13 Henderson Road Inverness

ISBN 0-86152-903-0

Acknowledgements

Since I first began working on this book, I have been indebted to many people for their generous assistance and encouragement. They have given time and typing, advice, encouragement, hints and stimulation which have all worked towards widening the scope of the anthology.

I must particularly thank Donnie M MacLean and the staff at An Comunn Gàidhealach (Stornoway office), Norman M MacDonald, Mairi MacDonald, Sheila MacLeod, John Murray, Donald S. Murray, Norman Smith.

Alasdair Smith has assisted as both co-editor and translator. Heather Delday and Roddy Murray have co-edited the photographic content.

Introduction

For over ten years I have been gathering poems which relate to
"The Long Island" of Lewis and Harris. This concept has an earlier
precedent in *An t-Eilean a Tuath*, a collection of songs edited by
Dòmhnall Iain MacLeòid (Glasgow 1972). *Siud an t-Eilean* concentrates
on contemporary poetry and takes its title from Donald MacAulay's
seminal study of the magnetic attraction and repulsion generated by
what lies between the Butt of Lewis and Rhenish Point.

The work is in Gaelic and English. It is by poets born on this island or
who live here or who have family background here, or who have been
driven to visit then stirred to speak by this geography and its community.

The clutter of books, photocopies, manuscripts and typescripts slowly
became a new, live book. The tones and viewpoints somehow cohere
despite, or perhaps because of, the disparate styles which express them.
The reader can counterpoint the vision of resident, exile and traveller.
I did not look for a theme but am amazed at how often shared concerns
and subjects straddle generations.

It has been equally rewarding to be trusted with new work by
established writers and with poems by those who are published here for
the first time. I have also been greedy, searching through many previous
publications for poems which refer with compulsion to The Long Island.
I gratefully acknowledge the work of many editors gone before.

There is no suggestion that Lewis and Harris form the centre of any
literary world or that the work the island motivates is in any way
superior to that brought to life by other islands – but there is a lot of
it. There is also an inevitable and healthy overlap with writing from
Skye and the Southern Isles. People born on one island live on,
or write of, another.

The photographs are also by "known" and "unknown" artists alike. There are all too many romantic images of the Hebrides available. It seems to me that all the photographers represented seek to reflect more than surface light. The emphasis is thus on people. As with the selection of poems, there was no editorial "policy" as to style. And again the varied work speaks by contrast. There are young and old people; town and rural images; the viewpoints of those who live here and those who travel here.

Some of these visual studies may shock those who do not expect the more "urban" side. There are no "retreats". This is a living island and where there is life there are tensions. I hope, however, that there is balance in the visual as well as the literary selection.

Some translations of songs and poems appear for the first time. When there has not been an available translation by the author, these have usually come about by a sort of animated committee of Gaelic specialists working with the editor.

This book could not have come about without the help of numerous advisors, particularly ones with a thorough knowledge of Gaelic language and verse, connotations and traditions. I regret that it is impossible to mention all by name.

And the book itself can never be comprehensive. I would have been happy to include one or two poets who declined to contribute. There must also be emerging poets I am unaware of. I hope someone will begin to gather a new collection from this or a wider or different group of islands. Until then, I hope that *There Goes The Island* speaks to you of life on a specific landmass which may be home to you or foreign ground. I trust that this collection can stir empathy.

Contents

Dàn 14 bho Il Maranzano

Ged a dh'fhalbh mi is ann leats' a tha mi fhathast,
tìr shlaodach na do shuidh' am measg nan tonn,
ann an uaigneas uasal;
is leòr dhuts' gnè nan ràithean anns a' ghaoith is an tuar
oir tha thus' mar sin air fad leat fhèin.

Bho trì àirdean bithidh thus', Trinacria,
ag amharc air fàire na cruinne
agus gun chobhair ag àrach mìorbhaillean is tìm.

Ar leam bhon bhroinn seo
nach eil mi a-muigh ach ann am pàirt
agus an dàn seo agam –
air ais is air adhart nam dhèidh –
gu h-eagarra sa bhùrn air mheidh,
crochte anns an t-saoghal.

Is ann annad a lorgar brìghean achrannach
nam beann,
innis searbh
agus tosd;
is os cionn gach nì osnaich bhan dorcha,
bàinidh dhìomhair
is bagairt ghruamach.

Is creag thu,
is oidhcheannan gorm thu,
is seinn an siocada fhèin thu.

Is tusa – far am fàs crann-ola agus bealaidh –
an làbha a lasas, an sgian,
an lann a bhoillsgeas,
coire anns a' chridh';
aithreachas,
is mathaid.

Francesco Maria Di Bernardo-Amato
(Eadar-theangachadh le Mìcheal Bartlett)

no. 14 from Il Maranzano

Though gone I am still with you,
slow land esconced among the waves, in aristocratic solitude;
for you suffice the wind-borne sense of seasons and their hues;

so are you quite alone.

From three points you view the globe's horizon,
Trinacria,
and aidless nourish prodigies and time.

It seems that from this womb I'm only part emerged
and back and forth must drag this half-birth's destiny;
precise in water, thus suspended,
balanced in the world.

You hide within you natures intricate
of mountain, bitter meadow
and of quiet;
and over all, the sighs of some dark women,
of arcane Furies
and tenebrous threat.

You are rock and water,
blue nights and cicada song;
you are the lava that ignites
the knife, the shining blade,
inhabited both by olive and by broom;
a fault within the heart;
perhaps remorse.

(Trinacria is an old Greek and Latin name for Sicily.)

Francesco Maria Di Bernardo-Amato
(translated by Michael Bartlett)

Clach an Truiseil

Bho chian tha mi an seo an sàs,
As mo bhun a' fàs am feur,
Nam sheasamh ann an cnoc na h-Aird
ag amharc àrd nan speur;
Is iomadh latha 's iomadh oidhch'
is linn a ruith an rèis
bho dhearc mi air a' Chuan a Siar
's struth Shiorramhaig na leum.

Ged 's iomadh stoirm len osag fhuar
Is gailleann chruaidh len gaoir
A shèid a-riamh orm mun cuairt,
Cha d' ghluais iad mi 's cha d' dh'aom;
Is mise gruagach an taoibh tuath
An eilean ruadh an fhraoich,
'S cha tàinig caochladh air mo thuar
No air mo ghruaidh mòr-aois.

Chì mi solas Nis ud shìos
Nuair laigheas grian an là,
'S chì mi sgoinn nan tonnan uain'
A' bualadh chreag gun tàmh;
'S gur tric tha sùil luchd-strì a' chuain
A chì mi bhuam gach tràt,
Gus an dearc iad fada bhuap'
Air gruagach ghlas na h-Aird.

Nuair thigeadh gruaim na h-oidhche teann
Is greann air feadh nam blàr,
Is an driùchd a' sileadh air mo cheann
Tha sealltainn do gach àird,
Is eòin nan creag air sgiath nan àm,
Nan deann gun ionad tàmh,
Gur tric ghabh fasgadh aig mo bhonn
An sprèidh bhiodh trom le h-àl.

Dearcaidh mi bho thaobh mo chùil
Air Mùirneag a' chùil duinn,
Is chì mi ceò gach feasgar ciùin
Ag iadhadh dlùth sna glinn;
Chì mi bhuam an t-arbhar làn
Air Mullach àrd an Tòil;
O, b' eòlach mi air tuar gach àit
Mus tàinig na tha beò.

Is iomadh neach bha eòlach orm
Tha nis air falbh gu bràth,
Cuid dhiubh cian an grunnd na fairg'
'S am Barabhas cuid nan tàmh;
Is cuid eile sgapte thall air chuan,
Is cuid bha cruaidh sna blàir,
Gu tric rinn sùgradh ri mo thaobh
'S air raointean glas na h-Aird.

Cò aig tha fios an ùin' a thriall
'S an cian a tha mi 'n sàs
Bho chunnaic mi air tùs a' ghrian
Cur sgiamh air feadh na h-Aird;
'S a-nis ged tha mo ghruag cho liath
A' faicinn triall gach àil,
An seo bidh mise gus an tèid
An cruinne-cè na smàl.

Murchadh Moireasdan

Clach an Truiseil

Who knows the age gone by,
The eternity I've seen
Since my first sight of sun
Shed green light on Ard.
Now I've gone grey,
Seen each race go by in dust,
I'll bide exactly here
Till earth dissolves in space.

And many a night and generation
Have run their span since
I saw further than Siorravig shore
To the Atlantic overfall.

Many's a gale and hurricane
Raged all about me,
Howling out with chill breath.
But I never moved.
Never yielded.

I'm the maiden of the North
In a brown island of heather.
No sign of dying on my face
Nor of ageing yet.

Butt of Lewis light in sight
At the lying of the sun
And green waves whetting white,
Restless, broaching rock.
Each day I watch the eyes
Of sea-strivers passing by
Seeking the grey maiden of Ard,
A shape from Shader's line.

Behind me I see the rise
Of Muirneag in the brown moor.
And in the calm of the dips
To the quiet evening mists,
Trailing shade over glens,
I've seen full harvests
Over Mullach an Toil.
I knew all that.
I knew it all
Before the living ones.

Murdo Morrison

Naoi Ceud Deug 's a Ceithir Deug

Nuair bhiodh òganaich cruinn,
Dhèanta grìosach bhuntàt':
"Siuthadaibh, seasaibh," siud chluinnt',
"Ach am faic sinn eil àird
A' mhailisidh nis oirnn –
'S gu Fort Dheòrs' thèid ma tha,
A mhailisidh an rìgh."

Dh'fhalbh mo ghràdh-sa Dimàirt
Do mhailisidh Fort Dheòrs',
Fèileadh-beag 's seacaid-bhàn
Air bidh 'n àit' pheitein-mhòir,
'S briogais thartain ghlan gheàird
Air an àit na tè chlò
Am mailisidh an rìgh.

"Cha bhi uat mi ach ràith,"
Thuirt e'n sgath bhlàth na cruaich –
Bidh mi còmh' riut, a ghràidh,
Mun tig càch às a' Bhruaich;
'S dòch' gum feuch mi mo làmh
Ann an gàrraidhean Chluaidh
Ma bhios rigears gan dìth."

Sheòl i, *Sìle* nan stuagh,
'S mòran sluaigh innt' air bòrd,
Cuid gu iasgach na Bruaich
'S tuath gu Sealtainn nan òb;
'S cuid a' falbh, mar mo luaidh,
A' chiad uair gu Fort Dheòrs'
A mhailisidh an rìgh.

Fhuair mi dhealbh an cèis dhùint'
'S chroch sa chùlaist le uaill
Agus litir ag inns',
"Tha gach nì dhomh cho nuadh.
Moch gar dùsgadh bidh phìob
Nuair is fìor throm ar suain
Am mailisidh an rìgh."

"On tha 'n cosnadh car gann,"
Thuirt e rium, "dhomh is fheàrr
Ghallaibh dhol nuair bhios m' àm
Anns a' champa seo 'n àird
Agus gabhail aig na Goill
Na mo chuibhlear am bàt' –
Seadh, ma ghabhas iad mi."

Naoi ceud deug 's ceithir deug,
Tigh'nn fo dhias nuair bha 'n eòrn,
Caismeachd airm, chualas cian:
Geilt is fiamh chuir e oirnn.
Teachd tha stoirm, dhubh e ghrian,
Mar bheul oidhch' rinn tràth-nòin,
'S e ri fògradh ar sìth.

Bhris an stoirm, 's an tuil dhòirt
'S air an Eòrpa rinn tigh'nn;
Tuil fhuil dhearg nam fear òg –
Seadh, fir òg nan ciabh mìn.
Thraogh is thràigh chun an fheòir
Fuil an cuislean 's an crìdh';
Dh'fhuairich, reoth 's chaill a clì.

Cuig a-riamh ghabh mo ghràdh
Tasdan eàrlais an rìgh?
'S gann gun bhris fo làn-bhlàth
'S bha sa bhlàr na thosd sìnt'.
Air a' bhuaidh 's daor a phàigh
Le fuil bhlàth dhearg a chridh
'S daor thu, bhuaidh, daor do phrìs.

Thuit blàth-bhraon air an raon
'S nigh aog-aodann nan òg;
Shèid a' chaomh-osag chaoin
Orr' is thiormaich is phòg,
'S i ri osnaich os cionn
Oigfhir ghrinn an fhuilt òir;
O mhailisidh mo chridh!

Colla, Fionnlagh is Dòmh'll
Ruairidh òg is Iain Bàn,
Aonghas, Uisdean 's Niall Mòr;
Chòrr cha shloinn mi am dhàn:
'N-dè nam balachain san dròbh –
'N-diugh gun deò anns an àr.
O mhailisidh mo chridh!

Tha chruach mhòna na luath,
Theich am fuachd, thill am blàths;
Thill luchd-cutaidh na Bruaich;
'S fhada buan leam tha 'n ràith
Gheall mo ghràdh bhiodh e bhuam
Aig a' chruaich 'n oidhch' a dh'fhàg –
O mhailisidh mo chridh.

Chaidh na geòidh tarsainn tuath,
Thug na geòidh mach an àil;
Thill gu deas mar is dual
Ard len àil air an sàil;
Ach cha till e, mo luaidh,
Ach nam bhruadar a-mhàin –
O mhailisidh mo chridh.

Murchadh MacPhàrlain

Nineteen Hundred And Fourteen

When we were young, we gathered,
Throwing potatoes to the late glow.
"Come on, stand," we would hear.
"Let's see how you measure up
Against the regulation mark.
If you reach it, it's Fort George."
The militia of the King.

My love enlisted on a Tuesday
In the militia in Fort George.
Dressed in kilt and khaki
To replace the wool jacket
And well-cut tartan trews
Instead of tweed homespun.
In the militia of the King.

"I'll be gone for one season,"
He said in shelter of the stack –
"I'll be back with you, my love,
Before the herring-girls return.
I might try my own hand
In the Clydeside shipyards
If it's riggers they're needing."

The *Sheila* took to the Minches,
Waving crowds on all her decks,
Some to the Broch fishing
Then the bays of Baltasound.
Some leaving, like my own love,
For the first time for Fort George.
The militia of the King.

I received his portrait, enclosed in a frame.
I hung it proudly, there in the recess.
And a letter telling,
"Everything is so new to me.
The bagpipes wake us early
When we're heavy with sleep."
In the militia of the King.

Nineteen hundred and fourteen.
Barley starting to blade.
Marching armies, at a distance,
Casting deep fear near us.
The storm coming, the sun black
Like a nightfall at noon.
To banish our peace.

That storm broke in red –
The flood upon Europe.
The deep blood of the young men,
Yes, the youth of the fine hair,
Emptied, ebbed in the grasses.
The blood from their arteries
Became a dead frost.

Till a warm-falling rain
Washed the soil from dead faces.
The breeze keening over them
Dried them as it touched them,
Yes, the youth of the yellow hair
And my own love
In his uniform.

The peat-stack is in ashes.
Cold and warmth took their turns.
The herring-girls came home.
Long for me is the season
My love promised he'd be gone
There at the peat-stack,
That night he left.

The geese went away to the north.
The geese, they hatched their young.
Returned south, in their due course.
But you will never return now,
Only in a dream to me,
Love, dead, in a uniform.

Murdo MacFarlane

22

An Cùlaibh Eirinn

Tha mi fo chùram an cùlaibh Eirinn,
Tha mi fo chùram air bòrd na h-iùbhraich
Is i gar giùlain a-null don Eipheit;
Tha mi fo chùram an cùlaibh Eirinn.

O, cha dìochuimhnich mi gu sìorraidh
Oidhche Chiadain an Iar air Eirinn;
Tha mi fo chùram an cùlaibh Eirinn.

An tè bh' aig fuaradh, an uair a bhuail i,
Bha cuid nan suain innt', 's cha d'fhuair iad èirigh;
Tha mi fo chùram an cùlaibh Eirinn.

Bha glaodh a' bhàis air gach taobh den bhàta
'S mo chridh' gu sgàineadh le cràdh gan èisdeachd;
Tha mi fo chùram an cùlaibh Eirinn.

Chithinn pàirt dhiubh le seacaid àrca:
Bha 'n fhairge làidir 's cha do shàbhail creutair;
Tha mi fo chùram an cùlaibh Eirinn.

Ach thèid gach cealgair a tha sa Ghearmailt
Chur sìnte marbh, bodhar balbh, gun èirigh;
Tha mi fo chùram an cùlaibh Eirinn.

Thèid Mussolini chur don a' phrìosan
'S le cromadh cinn cluinnidh e bhinn ga leughadh;
Tha mi fo chùram an cùlaibh Eirinn.

Thèid croich an òrdan is crochar beò e
'S bidh coin na Ròimh a' toirt fheòil o chèile;
Tha mi fo chùram an cùlaibh Eirinn.

Gach inneal marbhaidh a bh' aig a' Ghearmailt,
Bha siubhal na fairge is a' falbh nan speuran;
Tha mi fo chùram an cùlaibh Eirinn.

'Illean Leòdhais bha daonnan còmh' rium,
Bha Murchadh Sheòrais is Dòmhnall Sheumais;
Tha mi fo chùram an cùlaibh Eirinn.s

'S, O, MhicMhaoilein, gura tric mi smaoineachadh
Air bòidhchead d' aodainn 's do chaolas glè-gheal;
Tha mi fo chùram an cùlaibh Eirinn.

O, 'illean òga, nach tig sibh còmh' rium,
'S gun tog sinn tòrachd air chòir an treunas;
Tha mi fo chùram an cùlaibh Eirinn.

Tha mi fo chùram air bòrd na h-iùbhraich
Is i gar giùlainn a-null don Eipheit;
Tha mi fo chùram an cùlaibh Eirinn.

Ruairidh MacLeòid

West of Eire

I was heavy-laden, West of Eire,
On board our vessel, bound for Egypt.

When the one to our windward side was hit,
Those who were sleeping never woke.
Labouring heavily, west of Eire.

The death screams surrounding the vessel,
Tightening my heart to bursting point.

Catching sight of some in lifejackets,
But the swell was heavy and none was saved.

Mussolini will be put to the gallows
And his flesh fall to the dogs of Rome

The Germans might well be ground down
But I'll never forget that Wednesday night

Out there, west of Eire.
Join the pursuit in the cause of the fallen.
Heavy-laden, west of Eire.

Roderick MacLeod

Fo Sheòl

Bha 'm bàt' agam fo sheòl 's a' Chlàrach
ag gàireachdaich fo sròin,
mo làmh cheàrr air falmadair
's an téile 'n suaineadh sgòid.

Air dara tobhta 'n fhuaraidh
shuidh thu, luaidh, 'nam chòir
agus do ròp laist' cuailein
mu m' chridh' 'na shuaineadh òir.

A Dhia, nan robh an cùrsa ud
gu mo cheann-uidhe deòin,
cha bhiodh am Buta Leódhasach
air fóghnadh do mo sheòl.

Somhairle MacGill-Eain

Under Sail

My boat was under sail and the Clarach
laughing against its prow,
my left hand on the tiller
and the other in the winding of the sheet-rope.

On the second thwart to windward,
darling, you sat near me,
and your lit rope of hair
about my heart, a winding of gold.

God, if that course had been
to the destination of my desire,
the Butt of Lewis would not
have sufficed for my boat under sail.

Sorley MacLean
(Translation by the poet)

Neglected Graveyard, Luskentyre

I wade in the long grass,
Barking my shins on gravestones.
The grass overtops the dyke.
In and out of the bay hesitates the Atlantic.

A seagull stares at me hard
With a quarterdeck eye, leans forward
And shrugs into the air.
The dead rest from their journey from one wilderness to another.

Considering what they were,
This seems a proper disorder.
Why lay graves by rule
Like bars of a cage on the ground? To discipline the unruly?

I know a man who is
Peeped at by death. No place is
Atlantics coming in;
No time but reaches out to touch him with a cold finger.

He hears death at the door.
He knows him round every corner.
No matter where he goes
He wades in long grass, barking his shins on gravestones.

The edge of the green sea
Crumples. Bees are in clover.
I part the grasses and there –
Angus MacLeod, drowned. Mary his wife. Together.

Norman MacCaig

By the Graveyard, Luskentyre

From behind the wall death sends out messages
That all mean the same, that are easy to understand.

But who can interpret the blue-green waves
That never stop talking, shouting, wheedling?

Messages everywhere. Scholars, I plead with you,
Where are your dictionaries of the wind, the grasses?

Four larks are singing in a showering sprinkle
Their bright testaments: in a foreign language.

And always the beach is oghamed and cuneiformed
By knot and dunlin and country-dancing sandpipers.

– There's Donnie's lugsail. He's off to the lobsters.
The mast tilts to the north, the boat sails west.

A dictionary of him? – Can you imagine it? –
A volume thick as the height of the Clisham,

A volume big as the whole of Harris,
A volume beyond the wit of scholars.

Norman MacCaig

Below the Clisham, Isle of Harris:
After Many Years

On the mountain pass to Maraig
I met an old woman
darker but only just
than the bad weather we were in.

She was leading a cow by a rope
all the way round the mountain
to Tarbert.

She spoke to me in a misty voice,
glad to rest, glad to exercise
her crippled, beautiful English.

Then they trudged on, tiny
in a murky space
between the cloud of the Clisham
and a tumbledown burn.

And I suddenly was back home again
as though she were her people's history
and I one of her descendants.

Norman MacCaig

So Many Worlds

I stand for a few minutes
at the mouth of Hell's Glen.
Not because I think there are devils in it
and generations of the dead
being tortured for the sins they can't forget.

Behind me the loch I know so well
smiles in the sun and laughs along its shores.
It is part of my Paradise –
with not a saint in it
no harps twangling
their endless tunes.

Always between two worlds,
Hell's Glen and Paradise
and that's not counting those inside me –
where the moon brushes its way
through groves of birch trees
and ice floes ignore those silent dancers
in the midnight sky
and cities that have died
send their ghosts into the streets of Edinburgh
and the word she spoke changed my darkness
to a summer morning, friendly as a fireside.

Norman MacCaig

Leth-Cheud Bliadhna

Chaith mi spitheag
Air aghaidh fhèathach na mara
Is mi nam bhalach,
Is leum a' chlach thana, a' dannsa gu h-eutrom
Deich uairean – a-mach às mo shealladh –
Mus do shir i an grunnd.
Is mi a bha moiteil
A chionn nach do leum spitheag mo bhràthar
Ach a naoi ...

Chaidh mi air m'ais an-dè
Chun an aon chladaich
Is dh'fheuch mi spitheag
Mar a rinn mi leth-cheud bliadhn' air ais –
Clach chruinn thana
Air a taghadh gu h-ealant'
Bho chlachan a' chladaich
(Is an cladach air fàs cho salach
Seach nuair bha mi nam bhalach).
Ghabh mi cuimse air an sgeir
Far am biodh na faoileagan a' cumail
Coinneamh-ùrnaigh air Là na Sàbaid
Is cèilidh air làithean seachdain
Nuair bha mi nam bhalach.
(Cha chreid mi nach e taigh-fhaire
Bha aca an-dè –
Cha robh dad den t-seann lùgh nan guth.)
Chuir mi frasan smugaid air a' chloich
Mar a b' àbhaist dhomh a dhèanamh nam bhalach,
Mar a bhithinn a' faicinn m' athar a' dèanamh
Nuair bhiodh e ri taomadh
(Gus an do chuir mo phiuthar stad air
A' chiad uair a thàinig i air ais bho cosnadh.
– Tha mi 'n dùil gun do shaoil leatha
Nach robh e leòmach),
Is thilg mi an oileag le m' uile neart.
Thug i aon leum aiste
Mar gum biodh coineanach is urchair na mhàs,
Is sìos fodha mar steàrnan ag iasgach chudaig.
Aon spitheag an àite deich
– B' e sin mo thàmailt.

Nach iad na clachan a tha air fàs trom
Agus an cuan air fàs tana
Bhon bha mise nam bhalach ...

Ruairidh MacDhòmhnaill

Fifty Years

I threw a pebble
On the calm surface of the sea
When I was a boy
And the stone leapt and lightly danced
Ten times out of my sight
Before it sought the bottom.
How proud I was,
For my brother's pebble leapt
Only nine times.

I went back yesterday
To the same shore
And threw a pebble
As I did fifty years ago –
A round thin stone
Skilfully chosen
From the stones on the shore
(But the shore is so dirty
Since I was a boy).
I aimed at the rock
Where the seagulls kept a prayer meeting on Sundays
And ceilidhs on weekdays
When I was a boy.
(I think it must have been a wake
They held yesterday –
There was none of the old vigour in their voice.)
I spat on the pebble
As I used to do when I was a boy,
As I saw my father do
When he dug the lazy beds
(Till my sister stopped it
The first time she came home from service
– I think she did not consider
That it was proper),
And I threw it with all my might.
It gave one leap
Like a rabbit with a pellet in its bottom
And down it went
Like a tern fishing for cuddies.
One leap instead of ten
– Was I ashamed.

How heavy the pebbles have grown,
How thin the sea
Since I was a boy ...

Roderick Macdonald
(Translation by the poet)

Nuair a Thig an Dorch

Nuair a thig an dorch
ort, a' toirt air falbh Mùirneag
's Beinn Phabail is Hòl,
nuair a bhios do chaoraich 'nan laighe,
am feur dorch ann am brù na h-oidhche,
's a' ghealach ùr gun èirigh,
tilgidh mi 'n t-ultach mhònach-s' air an teine
's nì e solas.

Ruaraidh MacThòmais

An Eileatrom

Solas Airnis air mo làimh dheis,
Mùirneag fo bhrat,
cuibhrig air Beanntan Bharbhais,
anart air Hòl,
grèim againn air an eileatrom
's i tulgadh 's a' tulgadh air bàrr cuimhne.

Ruaraidh MacThòmais

When the Dark Comes

When the dark comes
over you, taking Muirneag away
and Bayble Hill and Hol,
when your sheep are lying,
the grass dark in the womb of night,
the new moon not yet up,
I shall throw this handful of peats on the fire
and it will make some light.

Derick Thomson

The Bier

Arnish light on my right,
Mùirneag cloaked,
a coverlet on the Barvas Hills,
a shroud on Hòl,
we grasp the bier-poles,
rocking and plunging on the surface of memory.

Derick Thomson

Air an Aiseig gu Leòdhas

A' leth-aithneachadh gach duine air a chuideachd,
aithne gun chuimhne,
is cuimhne gun aithne.
Tuigse a' tulgadh.
Tha am muir seo glas-
neulach, chan eil beatha
a' snàgadh tuilleadh bho na cladaichean,
tha am protoplasma
gun chumadh.

Ruaraidh MacThòmais

Anna Urchardan
a chaochail 11.3.87

Feasgar ann
's a' ghrian air cromadh,
blàthan na h-iadhshlait a' dùnadh
air aghaidh na creige,
's Loch Eireasort fo dhubhar
a' plapail air na leacan,
tha an geata
air iomall a' bhaile dùinte,
tha na caoraich
a' laighe sìos a chnàmh an cìre,
an Leathad Mòr fo raineach,
sàmhchair anns a' bhothaig,
gach creutair a' dol mu thàmh
na Cheòs fhèin –
bha là fad' agad
is làdach beatha
is thoill thu do dheagh chadal.

Ruaraidh MacThòmais

On The Ferry To Lewis

Half-recognising each by his kin,
a knowing-without-remembering,
and a remembering-without-knowing.
The understanding pitching.
This sea is grey-
filamented, no life
slithers any more from the shores,
the protoplasm
has no shape.

Derick Thomson

Ann Urquhart

Evening,
the sun setting,
honeysuckle blossom closing
on the rock face,
and Loch Erisort in the dusk
lapping the flat stones,
the gate
at the village boundary closed,
the sheep
are lying down chewing the cud,
the Big Brae under bracken,
quiet in the children's 'bothy',
every creature is going to rest
in its own nook/Keose –
yours was a long day,
with full pails of life,
and you have earned a good sleep.

Derick Thomson

*Ann Urquhart, who died in 1987, aged 86, was my mother's sister,
brought up in the little village of Keose. She served as Provost of
Stornoway and in many other capacities.*

Hòl, Air Atharrachadh

Is gann gu faca mi Hòl am bliadhna,
bha e air fàs cho beag;
feumaidh gu robh 'n Cruthaighear trang
leis an tarbh-chrann,
a' sgrìobadh a' mhullaich dheth
a bha cho àrd 's cho fionnar
's ga chàradh aig a' bhonn,
a' toirt air falbh a chaisead,
agus is dòcha a mhaise,
ga lìomhadh gus a robh a chruth
air a chall.

Air a neo
's ann ormsa bha E 'g obair.

'S mas ann
dè eile rinn E orm?

Ruaraidh MacThòmais

Hol, Changed

I hardly noticed Hol this year,
it has become so small a hill;
the Creator must have been busy
with the bulldozer
scraping away its summit
that was so high and so fresh
and depositing it at the foot,
robbing it of its steepness
and perhaps of its beauty,
smoothing it until its lines
were lost.

Alternatively
He was at work on me.

And if so,
what else did He do to me?

Derick Thomson
(Translations by the poet)

Do Mo Mhàthair

Bha thus' a' sgoltadh sgadain
ann a Yarmouth fad air falbh
's a' ghrian shaillt sa mhadainn
ag èirigh às a' chuan
's an fhuil air oir do sgine
's an salainn ud cho garbh
's gun thachd e thu o bhruidhinn
's gu robh do bhilean searbh.

Bha mis' an Obar-Dheadhain
a' deoghal cùrsan ùr',
mo Ghàidhlig ann an leabhar
's mo Laideann aig an stiùir,
nam shuidh' an siud air cathair
's mo chofaidh ri mo thaobh
is duilleagan a' crathadh
siùil na sgoilearachd 's mo thùir.

Tha cionta ga mo lèireadh
mar a dh'èirich 's mar a tha.
Cha bu chaomh leam a bhith 'g èirigh
ann an doilleireachd an là,
bhith a' sgoltadh 's a bhith reubadh
iasg na maidne air an tràigh
's am muir borb ud a bhith beucadh
sìos mo mhiotagan gun tàmh.

Ged a nì mi sin nam bhàrdachd
's e m' fhuil fhìn a th' air mo làimh,
's gach aon sgadan thug an làn dhomh
a' plosgartaich gun dèan mi dàn,
's an àite cùbair tha mo chànan
cruaidh is teann orm a ghnàth
is an salann garbh air m' fhàinne
a' toirt beothalachd don bhàs.

Iain Mac a' Ghobhainn

To My Mother

You were gutting herring in distant Yarmouth and the salt sun in the
morning rising out of the sea, the blood on the edge of your knife,
and that salt so coarse that it stopped you from speaking and made
your lips bitter.

I was in Aberdeen sucking new courses, my Gaelic in a book and
my Latin at the tiller, sitting there on a chair with my coffee beside
me and leaves shaking the sails of scholarship and my intelligence.

Guilt is tormenting me because of what happened and how things
are. I would not like to be getting up in the darkness of the day
gutting and tearing the fish of the morning on the shore and that
savage sea to be roaring down on my gloves without cease.

Though I do that in my poetry, it is my own blood that is on my hands,
and every herring that the high tide gave me palpitating till I
make a song, and instead of a cooper my language always hard and
strict on me, and the coarse salt on my ring bringing animation to death.

Iain Crichton Smith

Na h-Eilthirich

A liuthad soitheach a dh'fhàg ar dùthaich
le sgiathan geala a' toirt Chanada orra.
Tha iad mar neapaigearan 'nar cuimhne
's an sàl mar dheòirean,
's anns na croinn aca seòladairean a' seinn
mar eòin air gheugan.
Muir a' Mhàigh ud, gu gorm a' ruith,
gealach air an oidhche, grian air an latha,
ach a' ghealach mar mheas buidhe,
mar thruinnsear air balla,
ris an tog iad an làmhan,
no mar mhagnet airgeadach
le gathan goirte
a' sruthadh don chridhe.

Iain Mac a' Ghobhainn

The Exiles

The many ships that left our country
with white wings for Canada.
They are like handkerchiefs in our memories
and the brine like tears,
and in their masts sailors singing
like birds on branches.
That sea of May, running in such blue,
a moon at night, a sun at daytime,
and the moon like a yellow fruit,
like a plate on a wall,
to which they raise their hands,
like a silver magnet
with piercing rays
streaming into the heart.

Iain Crichton Smith
(Translations by the poet)

Lewis

It follows me, that black island without ornament,
which I am always questioning.
That wind on the headlands – is it really the exiles
keening homeward from abroad?
These daffodils,
are they the souls of the many dead?
Gaelic sings in my mouth. Its rainbow
arches the empty moors.
In black the old women walk
to the sparse and resonant church at evening.
The hills are bordered with blue.
In the stone cemeteries there are tales of sailors,
incised bibles, testaments.
The oil rig looms in the bay.
Wise maidens, which did you keep burning,
gold treasuries or poems?

In summer I have lain under the high sky
while butterflies wafted by
and the bees rummaged the buttercups
and on the horizon the slow ships passed
as in a frieze of blue.

Sea, immortal, waters, you are the harmony
around us forever.
We exist in your music,
in your blizzard of white gulls.

The helmeted mussels roost on the rocks,
crabs sidle through the pools,
the herring slide into the dangling nets,
and the humped seal turns away from land,
is transformed to a flirting lady.

Lewis, your sea, your exiles, your moons,
I sing of you each day.
Wherever I am, you are with me,
my music is the music of your stones,
your accordions
play in the autumn moons,
red and broody "bringing the exiles home."

You are the book
which I always study
in sunsets over the Minch,
you are my gaunt theme,
my poem
which burns in water.

You dance with the lost scholars,
the hives of theology,
and your yellow meadows
breed an anarchy of larks.
Dressed in a purple haze,
I come home to you
as a cow with milk
to the milkmaid in the evening.
The pail froths with warm foam.

Iain Crichton Smith

No 1 from 'A Life'

'When did you come home? When are you leaving?'
'No, I don't ... don't think I know ...'
The moonlit autumn nights of long ago,
the heavy thump of feet at their late dancing.
'We'll sail by the autumn moon to Lewis home.'
'I think I know you ...' But our faces age,
our knuckles redden and webbed lines engage
eyes that were once so brilliant and blue.
The sharp salt teaches us. These houses, new
and big with grants and loans, replace the old
thatched walls that straggled in a tall lush field.
I lie among the daisies and look up
into a tall blue sky where lost larks chirp.
The sea is blazing with a bitter flame.
'When are you leaving? When did you come home?'
The island is the anvil where was made
the puritanical heart. The daisies foam
out of the summer grass. The rigid dead
sleep by the Braighe, tomb on separate tomb.

Iain Crichton Smith

Garry Beach, Lewis

Bill Lucas

Sea wall at the Braighe

Iain Macleod

Storm at the Braighe

John MacKinnon

Na Marcaichean

Ciod iad an smuain, na fir bhrùit' air a' mhachair,
Nuair mharcaicheas Moloch a thogail na cìs?
E crathadh na srian 's cas na steud-each gan nighe
Am fuil nam fear gaisgeil nach marcaich a-rìs.

O, mharcaich sibh uile aig briseadh na faire
Thar chrìochan, thar bhailtean, thar chorp a tha breun;
Ach 'n do choinnich sibh fhathast ri marcaich' 's each geal aig'
'S e gun tròcair ag agairt a chòraichean fhèin?

Na fir ùra bu làidir', na braighdean bu tràilleil,
Na gaisgich san àr a bha dàicheil is treun,
Thàinig geilt air an aghaidh is shleuchd iad na làthair –
'O dìon on Each Bhàn sinn, 's am Bàs ruith na cheum.'

Cò dh'fhàg sinn 'n seo brùite, an dòrainn ar creuchdan,
Beum corran a mharcaich' ri fhaicinn nar crè?
Ciod dhuinne ged dh'aithriseadh càch ar cuid euchdan
'S ar mnathan 's ar leannain 's fear brist' aig gach tè?

Cailein T MacCoinnich

The Riders

What are their thoughts, the crushed men on the machair
When Moloch rides out to gather the tribute,
Bridle rattling and washing the charger's fetlocks
In the blood of the heroic, who will ride out no more?

You have all ridden at the breaking of watch
Over borders, habitations, over putrefying corpses,
But have you yet met a rider on a pale horse
Who, without mercy, pursues his own harvest?

The youth who were strongest, the most enslaved captives,
The heroes in battles who were fit, well-tempered,
Their faces showed terror, they knelt in his presence –
From the pale horse protect us, Death runs in his steps.

Who left us here crushed in the anguish of wounds,
The rider's sickle-cut to be seen in our frames?
What is it to us if all laud our valour
With our wives and our lovers left a broken man each?

Colin N Mackenzie

from 'In Memoriam'

From II: You Said

My Requiescat In Pace pyjamas, You said,
Are in the chest of drawers, second down
From the top, on the left – although, You said,
I have no serious objections to a shroud instead.
Will you sleep in this bed after I am dead?
Yes, I said – You smiled, very pleased:
That will be nice, You said. – Then:
I have been lucky, You said.

VI: Forlorn Hope

I shall drink from your cup tonight:
But tea, not coffee.
So that – who knows? – perhaps you might
Taste it with me.

Taste it with me though you be dead:
But yet so alive.
Though none shall see you bend your head
To touch the brim with me.

Then it may be that you will chance
To whisper a word –
And perhaps break this silence:
Le Silence de la Mort.

Only, I know, I know too well:
Now, and for ever,
The dead are dumb. They will not tell
That which we long to hear.

J. Mesleard

Inventory

Room
with a view.
Sea winds from the warm south.
Gutters
bathed in herring scales
turning
into sea-creatures
chattering in velvet Gaelic.
Brown sails
nudging wherries and drifters
into the crowded bay.
White-wood barrels
stand on each other,
eager for a glimpse
of the sea
which would carry them
to Danzig
and the Baltic Sea.
East-coast voices,
sharp and cutting,
sing a song of success.
Gaelic voices,
keen their survival,
at the strangers' behest.
Room
with a view
and the vista
of a child's mind.

Francis Thompson

South Beach Street

There is nothing left
now
of that four-walled space
which
was my first-world;
whose daylight
was a watery sun
blown by a sou'-westerly
and whose moonlight
was an oil-lamp
dripping
yellow
onto a bare table.
Thus far from then
the sou'-westerly still blows
chiller now with age.
Moonlight
is turned to sodium
to fill that empty space
and smother
the small cry
of the new-born.

Francis Thompson

Bread From Stones

I had read,
with disbelief,
how the islanders
on Irish Aran
made soil
from virgin rock.
That feat of creation
I now see
here in my own land.
Gods,
in their roles as crofters,
wrenched from their fertile lands,
combine an alchemic mixture
of dulse and sea-sand
and make
soil for growth.
Soon,
the Duke will come
to say:
'These people hungered.
I gave them stones.
Now look –
they have made bread!'

Francis Thompson

Mothachadh

A' chiad turas a bhuail orm
nach robh thu gu bhith buan
an latha samhraidh ud
ann an òr-bhlàth na Màighe
a thug sinn a' chlann leinn
air cuairt chun a' Bhràighe.

Iadsan fodha gu 'n iosgaidean
a' stialladh tron t-sàl,
glaodh an toileachais
riaraichte
tighinn gu m' chluasan
thar a' bhàigh.

Mis' nam shuidhe
ann an achlais do sgàile
crùbt' am fasgadh bruaich
a' maoidheadh oirnn gu h-àrd.
Thusa sìnt' nad shuain
os mo chionn air an tràigh,
sùil mo sgrùdaidh gad fhaicinn
fosgailt', ciùin, na do thàmh.

San anail sin dhearc mi
air gaiseadh nad shnuadh,
tainead bàsmhor do lethchinn,
dealt an fheòir air do ghruaidh;
dh'fhidir mi cràdh
nuair thionndaidh thu rium,
gath eagail gam sgàineadh,
deòir a' snàgadh nam chom.

Sheila NicLeòid
(Eadar-theangachadh le Sheila NicLeòid)

Inkling

The first time
I thought of you as mortal
Was the summer's day
We took the children
To the Braighe

They splashed in safety
Just beyond the long-toed tidemark
Their screams of pleasure
And satiety
Came back to me

I sat
Within the curve of your shadow
Couched in the shelter
Of the overhanging mound
You lay asleep above me
Open to scrutiny

And suddenly I saw
The hollow in the
Grass-dewed cheek
You turned to me
And felt the first
Stir of fear.

Sheila Macleod

Os Cionn Ròineabhal

Os cionn Ròineabhal
a' ghrian
'na craos bàndhearg
crochaicht,
am priosam sàil a' spreadhadh a solais
's mi falbh às an dùthaich.

Is ceistean a' brùchdadh gu brais,
a' bàthadh na ceist
a mhaireas
gus an tèid an lèirsinn a bhàthadh:

an saoghal à neoni air a' chiad latha?
às a' ghrèin?
à spreadhadh neochonbhallach
a shad e a-steach bho iomall a' chrios-reul?

An rathad a' snìomh caol romham
's às mo dhèidh
's mi a' siubhal,
le siab bho thuath gu deas
a' ghrian fhèin air bhogadan ...

Dè rèisde mu fhaireachdainn is tuigsinn?
An ceum bho mhòr gu mean?
Ciod as ciall do fhaicinn is neo-fhaicsinn?
Slàn is brist'?

A' siubhal bho àite gu àit eile
tha mi a' giùlan
far eil mi dol is far an robh mi –
mar sin ciod an difear eadar ionad agus slighe?

Is ciod as ciall don fhear-siubhail?
Falbhanach,
fear oir-iomallach?

Air cùl Ròineabhal
a' ghrian
'na cruinne spealgte
dol às
's mi fàgail mo dhùthcha.

Domhnall MacAmhlaigh

Roineabhal

Over Roineabhal
the sun
a white-red blaze
suspended,
the salt prism shattering its light
as I depart from my country.

Questions erupting swiftly,
to drown the question
that lasts
until insight is drowned:

the world out of nothing on the first day?
out of the sun?
from a random explosion
that tossed it in from the margin of the galaxy?

The road twisting narrowly before
and after me
as I travel,
swinging between north and south
the sun itself on a see-saw ...

What then about feeling and understanding?
The step from great to small?
What is the point of seeing and non-seeing?
Whole and shattered?

Moving from one place to another
I encompass
where I've been and where I'm going –
what then is the difference between place and journey?

And what of the traveller?
A wanderer,
a marginal man?

Behind Roineabhal
the sun,
a shattered world,
goes out
as I leave my country.

Donald MacAulay

Uilebheist

A leth-cheud bliadhna na ràithe sa
sheòl am *Metagama*,
shnàmh i air falbh bhuainn
'na bèist-mhara
a shluig ar gaisge 's ar n-òige.
Thog i cùrsa air nach ruigeadh fradharc,
gu grunnd air nach deargadh caoineadh.

On latha sin tha i daonnan
'nar bruadair,
ag eirigh air uachdar ann le uinneagan dealrach:
sgeadaicht an òran 's an uirsgeul,
duais na bochdainn
'na bun-dhealbh an lìon ar n-eachdraidh.

Tha sinn ga sìr-iarraidh
mar iuchair
a bheireadh fuasgladh do ar staid,
a bheireadh buaidh air sileadh ar brìgh,
ar dìmeas 's ar mealladh oirnn fhìn –
ar dòchas
air a' bhànaidh a' rannsachadh gach geodh'
eadar seo is Nineveh,
a' sìr-cheangal ri cladaichean ciana.

Chunnacas i am bliadhna rithist.
Tha na sanasan crochaicht ris na h-uinneagan.
Tha sgiobaidhean sianta gam fasdadh.
Is tha Ahab
ga bheartachadh fhèin chun an t-seilg.

Domhnall MacAmhlaigh

Monster

Fifty years this season
the *Metagama* set sail,
it swam away from us,
a sea-monster
that had swallowed our valour and youth.
It set a course the eye could not follow
to a ground where weeping would be in vain.

From that day it is constantly
in our dream,
it rises to its surface with bright-lit windows:
decked out in song and tale,
the reward of poverty
a base-motif in the web of our history.

We pursue it constantly
as a key
that would unravel our condition,
a remedy for the ebbing away of our worth,
for our self-derogation and our self-deceit –
our hope
obsessively searching every creek
between here and Nineveh
always confined to distant shores.

It has been sighted again this year.
The advertisements are posted on the windows.
Immune crews are being hired.
And Ahab
is girding himself for the hunt.

Donald MacAulay

Chan Eil Ann Cho Seòlta ris an Fhoghar

Chan eil ann cho seòlta ris an fhoghar
's am fonn air abachadh
gus teud thoirt beò anns a' cholainn
fathann air an t-slighe dhìomhair
infhios air a' cheòl a cheangleas
bith is bithbhuantachd

am baile is òr air
an coirce anns an adaig
an loch ri taobh na feannaig
'na sgàthan
dealbh an t-saoghail fhaicsinnich
an rathad ann 'na shnàithlean
a leanar gu iomall na dùthcha

gun chasg air aiseag
fiath air a' chaolas

ach uspag dhorch an t-sìl
a' cluich an uisge contraigh

fo shrian ùmhlachd

glagail air geòidh dhàna
ri dol air eilthireachd

fear a' sìneadh ceum iomganach
dhan choinneimh

mus tig an dùbhlachd.

Domhnall MacAmhlaigh

Strings

Nothing is as cunning as the autumn
the land tuned to ripeness
to activate a string in the body
a resonance of the hidden journey
an inkling of the music that relates
being and eternity

the village golden
the oats stooked
the loch beside the plot
a mirror
an image of the overt world
the road a thread on it
to be followed to the edge of the land

sea-crossing unhindered
the narrows calm

save the dark gust of the shoal
sporting in a slack tide

reined in obedience

bold geese belling
going on their pilgrimage

a man striding out anxiously
to the meeting

before dead of winter comes.

Donald MacAulay
(Translations by the poet)

Cladh Lochlannach, Na Hearadh

Air blàr na machrach seo
Chan eil leac na laighe
No clach-uaighe na seasamh
Ach na meallan lem flùraichean
Fhathast a' nochdadh nan làrach sin
A dh'fhag na cuirp a dh'abaich ann.

Tormod Calum Dòmhnallach

Bàtalosgadh

Cladach lom air eilean:
Ceò dhubh a' sruthadh bho bàta na teine.
Uair ann a dh'iasgaich na fir sin na broinn
Iad an dràsd a' tilgeil ola
Ri cur linn lasrach.

Faic iad ri falbh
Cinn crom
Làmhan paisgte ri dromannan crùbte.
An corragan corrach dùinte, a' siabadh bho chèile
Am brògan a' pronnadh a' mhoil ...
An deas-ghnàth seachad
Thèid iad dhachaigh.

Tormod Calum Dòmhnallach.
(Eadar-theangachadh le Tormod Calum Dòmhnallach)

Norse Graveyard – Harris

On the arena of this machair
Its grave slabs long scattered
Stand no ranks of memorial stones –
Yet grass cairns wink with flowers,
Still trace the patterns made
By their long greening dead.

Norman Malcolm Macdonald

Boatburn

Bare island beach:
Black smoke eddies from a burning boat.
These men once fished off her live frame
Now they heave lines of oil
Cast nets of flame.

Watch them walk away
Heads low
Hands folded to bent backs.
Scarred fingers clenched, they drift apart
Crunching the solemn stones...
The ritual done
They head for home.

Norman Malcolm Macdonald

Anna Campbell

Have you heard, an cuala sibh
The story of Brown-haired Allan and his Anna

It was from Stornoway that Captain Allan came
And his heart and mind were full
Full of Anna, Anna Campbell,
Anna Campbell from Scalpay,
Scalpay in Harris

We shall go on a sea journey
A sea journey from Stornoway to Scalpay
This is the way that Captain Allan sailed
To the island where he came to know Anna

This is my ship
A slim black ship of oak
Built in the town with money from the sea

There was great love between them
You understand
There was great love between Allan and Anna
And they had no fear
This being so, my friend, there being no fear
There was great love between them
Love cannot live where there is fear
Oh no

I have sailed as far as Spain

And home from Spain, Allan brings silk
Silk to bring gladness to Anna
Anna is an elegant girl
Will she not make clothes from the silk
Wedding clothes
Night clothes
Death clothes

This is the way that Allan took
But where is he going
To the espousal, the rèiteach
To harmonise the union
Between himself and Anna
Here is Anna
Waiting
Looking out for Allan's ship

I am in torment
No play tonight in my mind
The sound of the storm, the huge blasts

Brown-haired Allan, beloved of maidens
I heard that you went abroad
On the slim black ship of oak

You await Brown-haired Allan
O slim dark one
Standing down by the shore of Scalpay?

Not down on the shore
But up on this hill
Do I await my Allan's ship
It is here that I shall better see her
Moving down by the Enchanted Isles
Brown-haired Allan, I would go with you

Soon
And you shall have enough of the shore
My slim dark Anna
Enough
Do leòr

Brown-haired Allan, my beloved spouse
Young I gave you my esteem

Here comes the slim black ship of oak
Beating down by the Enchanted Isles

Brown-haired Allan, I would go with you

Listen!
The wind and sea are
Rising!

Look!
The mast is bending!

Look!
The sail is tearing!

The sail is gone

She is going down
Nothing can save her

O Mary mother
O Mary mother
O Mary mother

She is down
The slim black ship
Is gone

Tonight
My song is terrible
Not the death of cattle
But how wet your shirt is

The slim black ship is lost

Norman Malcolm Macdonald

Side Slipping

Iain Macleod

Kenneth, Vatisker, Lewis

Stornoway Girl   John Maclean

Am Bòla Beag

B' ann leatsa
Bha am bòla beag air an sgeilp
Oir ghabh thu còir air
Cheud là shìn thu mach do làmh:
"Faigh mi bòla eile dheth?"
Ceannruisgt' agus casruisgt'
Shuidhe tu
Aig a' ghrìosaich.

Dh'fhalbh thu uainn
Mar a dh'fhalbh do cho-aoisean eile
Nuair a chuireadh fios ort
Cha b' ann ceannruisgt' no casruisgt'
Agus
Cha b' e 'n bòla beag
A bha nad làimh
Ach Bìoball ùr
Agus sgrìobhte air an duilleig
An làimh sgrìobhaidh m' athar:
"Gum beannaicheadh Dia thu agus
Gun gleidheadh E thu."

Gun gleidheadh E thu ...

Thill do Bhìoball dhachaigh
An sgrìobhadh fhathast air an duilleig
Agus thill do ghuth:
"Faigh mi bòla eile dheth?"

Màiri NicDhòmhnaill

The Little Bowl

Yours
The little bowl on the shelf
You made it yours
The first day you reached out your hand:
"Another bowl of it?"
Barehead and barefoot
You sat
By the fire's heart.

You went from us
With your generation
When you were called.
Not bareheaded nor barefoot.
And
In your hand
Not the little bowl –
A new Bible.
Written on the white page
In my father's hand:
"Gum beannaicheadh Dia thu agus
Gun gleidheadh E thu."

"May he keep you ..."

Your Bible came back to us
The words still on the page
And you voice:
"Another bowl of it?"

Mairi Macdonald

Craobhan

Nach eil e iongantach
Gur anns na craobhan
A-nis tha bheatha.
Craobhan
Air an dlùth-chur
'S air fàs suas
A' mùchadh a' ghlinne
'S a' dubhadh na grèine.

Chuir iad às
Dha na caoraich.
'S tha an ciobair
Air fhògradh
Tobhta a shinnsrean
Fuar falamh
'S an gleann fo na
Craobhan.

Màiri NicDhòmhnaill

Trees

Is it not strange
That it is in the trees
There now is life
Trees
Planted close
Now grown high
Choking the glen
Darkening the sun.

The sheep
Are gone
The shepherd
In exile
The house of his forebears
Cold-empty
The glen under
Trees.

Mairi Macdonald

Crom-Lus Arrais

Bhuain mi crom-lus
An achadh arbhair
Faisg air Arras.
Fàilidh, dearg
Na bu deirge le
Todhar fala nam mìltean

'N ann an seo a thuit e?
Esan a bha mi sireadh.

Chum mi am flùr
Gu socair, maothail
An cuachadh mo làimh –
Buille chràitich mo chridhe
A' plosgartaich 's a' crith
Nam bileagan
Nis a' crìonadh.
Carson a spìon mi thu?
A dh'altram mi thu greis bheag
'S do fhreumhan fighte gu bràth
An duslach Arrais

Màiri NicDhòmhnaill

The Poppy Of Arras

In a field of corn
Near Arras
I picked a poppy.
Delicate, red,
Made more red
By the blood of thousands.
Did he fall here?
The one I was seeking.
I cradled the flower
Quietly, tenderly,
in the cupping of my hands –
The painful beat of my heart
Trembling and shivering
The petals
Now withering.
Why did I pluck you?
Nurse you for so short a time
When your roots
Are forever woven
In the dust of Arras.

Mairi Macdonald
(Translations by the poet)

An Toiseach

Nach neònach annas buaidh na cuimhne
nach ceadaich dhut a dhol nas doimhne
na chuibhreann sin nuair bha thu 'd naoidhean,
gun eadhan faileas deilbh nad inntinn
a-mhàin ort fhèin, no air a' mhuinntir
bha maille riut 's iad beò san linn sin?
's chan fhaigh thu cunntas ach tro chluinntinn,
's chan urrainn dhut gu bràth bhith cinnteach.

Dòmhnall Iain MacIomhair

A' Bhun-sgoil

Bàthte leis an t-sonas
tha mo chuimhne
air na leasain,
air an aibideil,
air a' chunntadh,
air dìth nan cùraman,
air na h-ùbhlan neochiontach,
air mìlseachd an rionnaich shaillte.

Dòmhnall Iain MacIomhair

The Beginning

Strange is the rarity of memory's effect
which permits you to go no further
than when you were an infant,
without a shadow of image in your mind
either of yourself or of those
who lived with you in that generation;
your knowledge is but what you hear
and you can never be sure.

Donald John Maciver

Primary School

Drowned in joy
is my memory
of the lessons,
of the alphabet,
of the counting,
of the apples of innocence,
of the sweetness of the salt mackerel.

Donald John Maciver

An Oige

Chuir mi car mun chnoc gu tùrail –
cnoc de chnuic am beanntan Uige
san àit' an d' rinn mo chuimhne dùsgadh;
feasgar Sàbaid shìos mun ghàrradh –
crìochan saogh'l le òrdugh màthar –
'g èisdeachd fuinn nan salm a' teàrnadh
togt' air bilean sluaigh an àirde;
a' call nan cas am measg na luachrach,
cha robh daorach 's cha robh buarach
a' bacadh adhartas na h-uarach,
ach bha sìth ann is bha fois ann,
is bha saorsa 's cead mo chois ann,
is bha ùrachadh 's gach frois ann;
ceòl is driùchd 's bu lìonmhor spòrsa,
sin cuimhneachan air cuairt na h-òige.

Dòmhnall Iain MacIomhair

Youth

Purposefully I went round the hill –
one of the hills of the mountains of Uig
in the place where my memory awoke;
on a Sunday evening down by the dyke –
the limit of my world on mother's orders –
I listened to the psalm tunes escaping
raised on the lips of people;
losing my feet among the rushes,
neither fetter nor intoxication
delayed the progress of the hour,
but there was peace and there was calm,
and there was freedom to move,
and refreshment in every shower;
music and dew and fun in abundance,
that is the memory of the cycle of youth.

Donald John Maciver
(Translations by the poet)

Callainn

thog mi
air ionnairidh Ghàidhlig
an snaim a bh'aig Fionn
air na coin
air iall a' sireadh
bithbhuantachd sgeòil.

is dh'ionnsaich mi
air latha-sgoile Beurla
nach robh ann ach creathall-chat
rud a dh'altaicheadh ar meòir
is a chuireadh ùine seachad.

o, bha mi nam shìneadh sa chreathaill
ach a-nis tha an ùine fàs teann
is mi sreangte
ann an lùb-ruith metaphor
cù gu cat
thar amall na meadhan-oidhche.

Iain Moireach

A' Bhliadhna Ur

An i seo a' bhliadhna
a leaghas na bodaich-shneachda
ann am pòg mhilis an t-samhraidh,
a ghairmear air na bodaich-starraig
taghairm nan trì gairm,
a thèid na leth-bhodaich
an spealgadh ri na cladaichean?

O chan i chan i.
Seasaidh na bodaich-shneachd
smèididh na bodaich-starraig
seinnidh na leth-bhodaich
dìreach mar a chleachd –
feumaidh a' bhliadhna dhol 'na cèis
is tha na cèisean gun mhùthadh.

Iain Moireach

Hogmanay

in evening Gaelic
I picked up
the knot Fionn used
for leashing
hounds that sought
stories beyond time

in schoolday English
I was taught
to call it a cat's-cradle
a looping exercise
to finger time away

yes, I rocked in that cradle
but now that time becomes tight
I am strung
in a metaphor's slip-knot
dog to cat
across the swivel of midnight

John Murray

The New Year

Will this be the year
that the snow-men melt
in the sweet kiss of summer,
that the oracle of three cries
will be invoked against the crow-men,
that the mutchkin-men
will be shattered on the shores?

O no it is not.
The snow-men will last,
the crow-men will wave,
the mutchkin men will sing
just as they have before –
the year must fit its shell
and the shells are immutable.

John Murray

Air Machair Bharabhais

a' ghaoth
a' siabadh na gainmhich
a' feannadh na machrach
ag ìsleachadh cnuic
ar n-eachdraidh
gu rannsachail gu fàsach

rabaidean èasgaidh
ag àiteach agus ag àrach
far na thogadh ar sinnsir
is far an deach an càradh

an cinn-san an-diugh
a' sgàineadh uachdar
mo sheallaidh
aiseirigh na bochdainn
gun dùil rithe

Iain Moireach

Deireadh Foghair

Bha a' ghealach ìosal trom
a' danns air a' mhonadh
a-raoir
ach crochait liath-bhàn
os cionn Bàgh Chròic
sa mhadainn.

Agus mise ri crìonadh
ann an conntràigh na fala
nam fhradharc na geòidh ghlasa
a dh'èirich às m'inntinn ...
còig sleaghan dhiubh
a' fiaradh is a' casadh
a' tarraing an eachdraidh
is a' coileanadh an dàn
air leacann chiùin an adhair.

Iain Moireach

Barvas Machair

the wind
sweeping sand
flays the machair
reduces the hills
of our history
winnowing to desert

eager rabbits
cultivate and breed
where our ancestors were reared
and where they were interred

today their heads
crack the surface
of my vision
miserable resurrection
unforeseen

John Murray

Late Autumn

Perfect and low the moon
danced on the moorland
last night
but hung pallid
over Croic Bay
in the morning.

I also wane
in the blood's neap tide
in my sight the grey geese
that arose from my mind
five lances of them
slanting and turning
drawing their history
rounding out their fate-poem
on the calm slopes of the sky

John Murray
(Translations by the poet)

The Well

I climbed over barbed wire to get to you,
I broke through several spiders' webs.
In one upward step, I spanned the rock I used to slide down.
There was no path left, or right –
But I went straight to you.

I could not see you for growth,
I tore away the fern and bailed you
Until you were almost empty,
Then I scrubbed you and dried you out.
Four hours, they said, and you would be full again.

The mist was heavy over all,
Blocking out the past, the future and almost the present –
An unattached bleat was the only sound.
At four o'clock the mist had risen, partly,
Part of the past was present,
But there was a slight scum on your surface,
So I bailed you out again.

At eight I could see the grey coast,
A new house going up, a boat or two,
The fallow lazy-beds.
The mist was almost gone then
And you were almost pure.
I took two pails of your water home.
And they said I was a fool.

Dolina Maclennan

At the Fank, Scarista, Harris

John Charity

Billy and Sharon, Harris

Beka Dilworth

Daoine Bha an Leòdhas Uaireigin

Bu mhìorbhaileach na daoin' iad,
Oighrichean acrach nan cruadalan.

Air an gineadh am bolg saillt na fairge,
Bu neo-thruacanta chaidh an snaidheadh
A creagan greannach an coimhearsnachd.

Air an altram an uchd farsainn a' chruthachaidh,
Bu luath a dh'fhoghlaim iad a dòighean
An oilthigh a cunnartan:
Bu chabhagach am fàs gu fearalas.

Bu tapaidh treun-fèithichte na gàirdeanan
A chreach liosan uisgeach a' ghrunna.

Bu theann an greum-tachdaidh a rinn iad
Air sgòrnan neo-ghealltanach an cuibhrinn,
A' fàsgadh às dòchas is aran;
(Tro stoirmean fallasach am beatha
Bu tric bha gach cuid dhiubh a dhìth orr').

B'fheàirrd' oighrichean sochaireach am buaidh,
Peann cruaidh an duinealais smiorail
A sgrìobh an cliù cinnteach le onair
Air cladaichean fiadhaich Leòdhais.

Calum Greum

People Who Were Once on Lewis

They were startling people,
The hungry heirs of hardship.

Cast in the salt gut of the ocean,
They were pitilessly pounded from
Their domain of grim rocks.

Reared on creation's wide lap,
They fast learned its ways.
In that university of dangers,
They were forced to boldness.

Brawny and taut-sinewed the arms
To plunder the watery garden of the sea-bed,
Taking an unrelenting stranglehold
On their thin, unpromised portion,
Wringing, through the sweating storms
Of their lives, hope and bread.
Often they went without either.

Their heirs benefit from their overcomings.
The hard scratching pen of bone
Marked their honourable thriving
On the wild shores of Lewis.

Calum Graham

The White Stone of Lewis

Do not attempt
to lift the white stone.
It is smooth quartzite
and weighs a lifetime.

You would prove your back
could take the strain;
brave, ambitious
you could handle any challenge.

But another strength is more sustaining:
able to change and take changes
lift old habits from heavy soil
get to grips with the stone surface
of self-deception.

Let those do the heaving and shoving
who shoulder burdens they cannot manage
and set their sights on defeating others
in aimless shows of strength.

You carry the stone within you
light with humour
crystal with hope
smooth with complete integrity.

Tessa Ransford

Tweed threads being delivered to a home-weaver, near Shawbost, Lewis, 1992

Jeremy Sutton Hibbert

Spinning the threads, Kenneth Macleod Mills, Shawbost, Lewis, 1992

Jeremy Sutton Hibbert

Johina Macleod does her washing. Shawbost, Lewis, 1992

Jeremy Sutton Hibbert

Harris Festival

tangles wrap rock
fade but insinuate
glaring pattern

tape or rope bleach
to seep out reds
can't match dulse

Ian Stephen

Harris Haiku

flood then seeping ebb
rut their own Sound of Kearstay
thrust their waters through

and when tides wear round
inconstant oppposition
confronts the wind drift

Ian Stephen

Fèis Na Hearadh

Snaim-cruimean mun chreag
a' crìonadh 's a' brosgal
eiseamplair làidir.

Sìoman a' gealadh
a' call dearg
nach fhaigh buaidh air duileasg.

Ian Stephen

Haiku Hearach

Lìonadh 's a' tràghadh
na h-uisgeachan a' sruthadh
tro Chaolas Ceartaigh.

'S nuair a thilleas an sruth
bidh còmhstrì neo-bhunailteach
an aghaidh na gaoith.

Ian Stephen
(Eadar-theangachaidhean le Alasdair Mac a' Ghobhainn)

Sealladh

Oidhcheannan Sàbaid samhraidh.
Walsal aig an t-seinn mu dheireadh.
Làn san fheur.

A' coiseachd gu taighean.
Sa bhàgh bha na sgeirean falaichte,
bàthte is fo sheun.

Suipear gun feum air solas.
A' cluinntinn thrìlleachan 's fhaoileag
's an t-anmoch 'nan sgiamh.

Iain MacDhòmhnaill

View

Sabbath nights in summer.
Walsal the tune at the last singing.
High tide up to the grass.

Walking to houses.
In the bay the reefs were hidden,
drowned and under a spell.

Supper with no light needed.
Hearing oyster-catchers and seagulls
with lateness in their cry.

Ian MacDonald
(Translation by the poet)

At Home

Darkening by nine in late August
but the western sky white
with a lurid gleam

Tall, inevitable stand the poles –
electricity, telephone –
and beyond them, around them,
between them
the thousands of fence-posts, gates,
wire new or rusty,
an island littered, enclosures enclosed
and enclosed again

I lead the cow
out by one gate, in by another.
Her familiar scowl, her breath
which is sour yet not unpleasant
completely. Tonight the moon full
and the bay a mould
in which the tide is swollen.
The west wind opposes its current
at turning

The land darkens quickly, night comes.
The hill has lost nearly all
its colour, on its dull surface
sheep lie like stones.
One bold lamb on the skyline

Ian MacDonald

Whale Rescue, Dalbeg

John Mackinnon

Sam Maynard

Mussel Raft, Loch Roag

On yacht 'Solus' bound for Rhenish Point

Ian Stephen

A High Blue Day on Scalpay

This is the summit of contemplation, and
no art can touch it
blue, so blue, the far-out archipelago, and
the sea shimmering, shimmering
no art can touch it, the wind can only
try to become attuned to it
to become quiet, and space itself out, to
become open and still, unworlded
knowing itself in the diamond country, in
the ultimate unlettered light

Kenneth White

from "Letter from Harris"

3.
Rodel
where the young men
built the beautiful ship
that the sea coveted
and the 'great cleric' lived
who founded the grammar school in Paris
Rodel this evening
is an empty harbour
a rusty iron ring
and a heap of red seaweed.

9.
'We think
of these northern islands
as storm-bound and mist-wrapped
yet nowhere
can there be greater
brilliance of colour
the sea so blue
the rocks so vivid
with saffron lichen

A meadow of sea pink
in June
contains all colours
between white and deep purple
and the white-feathered birds
reflect the boreal intensity
of the summer light'

10.
Medusae
on the white sand beach:
colour of brandy and whisky
or again
infinitely pale –
like the first clutch of living jelly
in a darwinian dawn

Kenneth White

A' Chlach

suath mi, a ghaoithean, le
naidheachd às gach àirde: sìn orm

suath mi, a ghrèine, do
shoillse teas mo chridhe: sìn orm

suath mi, a ghealaich, mo
leigheas na do ghilead: sìn orm

suath mi, a shiantan, ur
frasan ga mo nighe: sìn orm

tamh annam,
sàmhchar

Aonghas MacNeacail

The Stone

stroke me, winds, with
news from each quarter: rest on me

stroke me, sun, your
light heats my heart: rest on me

stroke me, moon, my
health in your whiteness: rest on me

stroke me, elements, your
showers wash me clean: rest on me

peace in me,
silence

Aonghas MacNeacail
(Translation by the poet)

What's Done Cannot Be Undone

The tide crawls forward now
washing the beach more thoroughly
than might seem necessary.
One wave, I think, would be enough;
but, obsessed, the scrubbing arm
sweeps round wide arcs of foam.
Returning water files through crevices
and shakes out weed to lay it slanting seaward.
It polishes, repeatedly; meticulously dries
already spotless sand. You might think it erased
an army's footprints, or deodorised
the bed of a mass orgy.
But almost no-one has been here.
A gull or two flew down and stood about;
a chain of three-toed tracks
wavers along the shore.
Last night an otter scurried round the rocks
and ran into the sea.
Perhaps a few small, necessary murders –
such as maintain the world – have taken place:
nothing that warrants this
fanatical twice-daily cleanliness
of waves destroying evidence of guilt
but not the spot itself. And waves forget
that they have washed all proof away.
Only their own faint, overlapping tracks,
like tiles laid upside-down, remain.
So, tirelessly, the tide begins again.
Last Winter, not remarkable for storms,
it scoured a beach of sand away.
The sea lathers my feet. As I step back,
it sets to work on my few idle marks.

Anna Adams

Iain Macleod

Drawing a Blank

Playground at 'Colditz' Stornoway

Barbara Ziehm

Funeral in Ness

John MacKinnon

Borgh Leòdhais

1.

Eaglais le uinneagan dathte
ri taobh an taigh againn. Eaglaisean
an àiteachan eile, òrdaighean
anns na h-eaglaisean. Ministearan
ann an aodaichean dubha,
busaichean a' tighinn o na h-òrdaighean,
agus sinn a' seinn shalm. Eildearan
ag ùrnaigh 's a' gàireachdainn ...
agus cailleachan ann am beannagan
aig bòrd a' chomanachaidh.
Taighean geala agus taighean dubha,
tidsearan le strapaichean,
uèirichean an teileafon,
agus Disathairne à Steòrnabhagh
drungairean air busaichean,
agus aon rud nach dìochuimhnichinn –
briosgaidean Ròigean, tioram, neo-mhilis,
cho cruaidh ris na crùbagan.

2.

Tha a' mhuir a' seinn an àiteigin,
tha mi a' cluinntinn a monmhar;
fada shìos air cùl nan gàrraidhean,
cho sòlaimte ri òrgan,
a' còmhradh, a' gàirich.

Maoilios M Caimbeul

Borve, Lewis

1.

A church with stained glass
beside our house, churches
in other places, communion services
in the churches. Ministers
in black clothes,
buses coming from the communions,
and we singing psalms. Elders
praying and laughing ...
and 'cailleachs' in kerchiefs
at the communion table.
White houses and black,
teachers with belts,
telephone wires,
and on Saturday from Stornoway
drunkards on buses,
and one thing I couldn't forget –
Ròigean's biscuits, dry and unsweet,
crab-hard.

2.

The sea sings somewhere,
I hear its murmur;
far away behind the walls,
solemn as an organ,
conversing, roaring.

Myles Campbell

Dathan a' Ghràidh

1.
Tha am baile cadalach, donn,
am monadh timcheall air
a' sìneadh gu fàire,
gu beanntan Na Hearadh.
Bhitheadh cliabh air na tuim,
cliabh nach eil beò an-diugh.
Ach a bheil e gu diofar
cò gheibh sealbh air an t-samhla seo,
ma tha gràdh anns a' chridhe?
'S a bheil e gu diofar
airson Shasannach is Eòrpach?
Cha sheachain an cridhe fàs
le siubhal gach latha,
a' ghrian ag èirigh 's a' laighe
air na feithean purpar.
Dè ged nach biodh Gàidheal idir ann –
an tigeadh seargadh air an fhraoch?

Ann an eilean eile – ann am Muile –
tha am monadh dosrach fhathast
agus corra Ghàidheal ga fhaicinn
a' fàs ris na srainnsearan.
Cha bhrist deur no dhà an aoibhneas-san –
's dòcha mar aoibhneas a' chiad Ghàidheil
a' faicinn Beinn Talaidh is Beinn Mòr
le còta òigheil a' gheamhraidh.

Chunnaic am fearann seo cuideachd,
lom 's gu bheil e,
iomadach beatha is bàs,
gus a bheil e 'n-diugh
sàmhach,
còmhnard gu fàire
mar dhàn donn do-thuigsinn.

Maoilios M Caimbeul

Love's Colours

1.
Drowsy village surrounded
by brown moor
to the horizon, to the Harris mountains.
There was a creel on the hillocks,
a creel no longer living.
But does it matter
who inherits this symbol,
if there is love in the heart?
And does it matter
for the English and those from Europe?
The heart must grow
with each day's decease, the sun rising and setting
on the purple fens.
Would it matter if there were no Gaels –
would the heather wither?

In another island – in Mull –
the moor blossoms yet,
with a few natives watching
it growing with the strangers.
A tear or two will not deter their joy –
perhaps like the joy of the first Gael
on seeing Ben Talaidh and Ben More
with their virgin winter coat.

This land also saw,
bare though it is,
death and life,
until it is today
silent,
smooth to the horizon
like a brown inscrutable poem.

Myles Campbell
(Translations by the poet)

Seceder Girl

After a day on the bare bones of hills
we reached cubes of stone,
the houses and four strips of croftland.
We knocked and they brought us in.

Neil's mother, beating cream in a churn,
kept up a thump like a tune in the kitchen.
Our friend took us through to the best room
to meet his sister, home from the mission.

Newly returned from the Holy Land,
her smile soft as wool of wethers,
she sat with us in her black twinset.
We were the same age, all young.

She had skin to see through, blue-dark hair
like a wing, words clean as quills;
her body concealed and subjected
in order to advance the spirit.

While she spoke she made the day
of the seven elements seem close.
Will city girls be sparks in that wintry wind
and she a slow-match burning on to the very end?

Valerie Gillies

Writer's Block

This white page
condemns my brain
to clumsy contortions,
while the few words
left in my stunted vocabulary
grate uneasily against each other
like empty bottles in a slack tide.

Where have they gone,
those words which crisply catch
meaning and intention,
distil feeling
and transmute groping thoughts
into rich implication?

The baleful stare
of this virginal face
yields nothing to my fumbling images
and unsure syntax.
There is no giving
in this cold companion.

Angus Macmillan

Psalm Moment

The rain had come,
was falling across the loch,
as light had fallen on us.

We lay down at the crossroads,
and all who gazed up
remembered their own psalm
in the falling of hills into hearts,
in the twice-born light of that ending day,
in the hand holding
a crying hill.

Steve Moore

Aignish on the Machair

Eyebright and yarrow,
bedstraw and stonechats.
I walk with high footsteps
to avoid the wet buttercups.

Over the rylock
Jon Hearach's man chips at a monument.
Plastic roses fade in clipped grass.

Behind the old yellow lichen
the stones are askew.
A soldier stands to attention
against the church wall,
feet turned in profile
like an Egyptian.

Did they need a Hearach then
to carve the Lewis dead?
Does the old rivalry
end at the gates?

I climb the stile to the car
and take the long road to Tarbert.

Morag Henriksen

Fithich

Ann an imnidh na maidne
tha iad air iteig gu socair,
a' cuartachadh 's a' cuartachadh
os cionn na mòintich.

Fithich chràbhach
ag ràdh na conaire gairge ud
airson nam marbh ana-creideach.

Fithich fhrithealach
nan sagartachd dhubh,
a' cuartachadh 's a' cuartachadh
anns an adhar throm,
a' toirt tròcair is ìobairt gu coma
don mhòintich.

Dòmhnall Rothach

Bithidh an Raon air a Tuileachadh

Bithidh an raon air a tuileachadh le feur ùr
is an raineach a' luasgadh
mar fheamainn anns an t-sùmainn.
Bithidh siùil gheala nan sgìtheach
air an togail ris a' ghaoith,
agus lusan beaga, buidhe is geala
a' dealrachadh
mar choinnle-Brianain anns a' ghuirme.

Slaodaidh a' ghrian reothart
thar gàrradh liath na raoin;
am measg nan craobh crìon cnàmhach,
bolg reothairt san aimsir mhàithreil;
reothart gàirdeach feòir ùir.

Dòmhnall Rothach

Ravens

In the disquiet of the morning
they are restfully on the wing,
circling and circling
above the moor.

Devout ravens
saying that harsh rosary
for the faithless departed.

Officiating ravens
in their black priesthood,
circling and circling
in the heavy sky,
bringing mercy and sacrifice indifferently
to the moor.

Donald Munro

The Field Will Be Flooded

The field will be flooded with fresh grass
and the bracken waving
like seaweed in the surge.
The white sails of the hawthorns
will be hoisted to the wind,
and little flowers, yellow and white,
glittering
like phosphorescence in the green.

The sun will drag a springtide
over the grey dykes of the field;
amongst the withered bony trees,
the swollen belly of springtide in the mothering season;
a joyful springtide of new grass.

Donald Munro
(Translations by the poet)

Bodach an Stoirm

(from Achiltibuie, last century)

Tell me the fishermen were drunkards or liars,
describing how, windward to Tanera,
the storm shook a creature loose
which shook their boat like a herring creel.
They called their rust-red leviathan
the "old man of the storm."

Just a daily fact
to a Macleod or Fraser,
Sinclair or Mackenzie.
As true as a good rope,
a taut sail, or a well-mended net.

Men who could read the stars
could also read the depths.
They named, like Adam,
the unknown in terms of what they felt ..
They considered the poet's "Kraken"
too grand a word for a splintered keel
or a shredded net
or the ridicule their tale
met with in Stornoway.

Tom Bryan

Travelling People, Harris 1975

I traded bread for a tin lamp
and welcome cup of tea.
We poked the ashes of the fire,
in parlay.
I traded the vineyards of California
for the salmon of the far pool.
An old woman burst from the birch tent,
shaking her fist, cycling over the moor for tobacco.

Whispering children came forth
to bounce some laughter off
the wind and rain,
their eyes mocking my own
which stung from
their warming fire.

Tom Bryan

Leanabh a' Tilleadh Dhachaigh

Air an aiseag
tilleadh dhachaigh
chi mi baile tron a' cheò
baile beag as aonais rathaid
taighean grànda dorcha.

Dè am baile
cò tha fuireach
is cuin is càit na dh'fhalbh iad?
Clachan mòra anns a' bhall' ud
ach chan eil iad àirde.

'S fhad an t-saoghail bho bha teine
anns a' chagailt fhuar sin;
ma bha clann a' cluich ball-coise
càit robh àite còmhnard?

Càit robh sgoil ac'
's robh iad toilicht'
bhith cho fad' air falbh bhuaip';
is dè a bh' aca airson siubhal
mur robh ann ach bàta?
An d'fhuair iad teilidh
no dè cho fada
's a bh' aca muigh sa gheamhradh?

Air an aiseag
tilleadh dhachaigh
bho na laithean-saora
baile beag as aonais rathaid
's cha robh duine beò ann.

Màiri NicGumaraid

124

Child Returning Home

On the ferry
returning home
I can see a village through the mist
a little village without a road
horrible dark houses.

What village is it?
who lives there?
When did they go, and where?
Big stones in that wall
but they're not high.

It's a long time since there was a fire
in that cold hearth;
if there were children playing football
where did they find level ground?

Where was their school
and were they glad
it was so far away from them?
And what did they travel in
if there was only a boat?
Did they get a telly
or how long
could they stay outside in winter?

On the ferry
returning home
from holiday
a little village without a road
and not a living soul in it.

Mary Montgomery

An Taigh-Tasgaidh 's an Leabhar

Feumaidh mi dhol chun taigh-tasgaidh
dh'fhaicinn uidheaman m' eachdraidh
a shad mo sheanmhair às
a shuath mo sheanair
le bhoisean cnapach sgìth
air a' chuairt mu dheireadh
a ghabh e
dhan t-sabhal.

Feumaidh mi dhol chun taigh-tasgaidh
as aonais duslach an fheòir
air m' aodach,
dh'fhaicinn uidheaman m' eachdraidh
mus tèid an leth-shealladh
den leth-sgeul
a th' agam
a dhìth
leis an sguab th' air cùl mo shàil.

Feumaidh mi leabhar bhith deas air mo shùil
de bhriathran nan làithean a dh'fhalbh,
feumaidh mi leughadh fa chomhair an àm
tha cànan an cunnart dhol balbh.

Feumaidh mi leabhar a dh'innseas dhomh sgeul
nach eil idir air bilean an t-sluaigh,
a dhol gu fear eile 'son barrachd de dh'fhios
's de thuigse air adhbhar na truaigh'.

Màiri NicGumaraid

The Museum and the Book

I must go to the museum
to see the tools of my history
my grandmother threw out
my grandfather stroked
with his tired knobbly hands
on the last round
he made
of the barn.

I must go to the museum
without the dust of the grass
on my clothes
to see the tools of my history
before the half-sight
of the half-story
I have
is swept
away by the brush at my heels.

I must have a book for my eyes
of the words of days gone by,
I must read it when facing the time
a language threatens to go dumb.

I must have a book that will tell me a story
that's not on the lips of the people,
must go to someone else for more information
and understanding of the reason for grief.

Mary Montgomery
(Translations by the poet)

Singing in the Ash-Heap

wearing faded black canvas on her feet
she called sandshoes
never taken to the only sand she ever saw
to run in
on Sunday School outings by the Atlantic
or when vanloads of visiting relatives
from away
made a strange thing called a day of it
at the seaside
which didn't have fairgrounds and ponies
like the pictures in the books

and dug the toes of the faded black into the brown
tan orange landscape
debris of months of peat
roughed about with egg shells and potato peel
and matchsticks and fishbones
and shooed the hens away
and made up tunes
to pass the time
in patterns to match
rain ridges in the ash

Mary Montgomery

Always in pairs

First winter days enter every crack;
Clean as metal, fresh from the press.
No promise of opulent summer here;
Disease died with the flowers.
Swans take my heart without asking;
Take it away, I don't know where,
Always in pairs, always in pairs.

Janice Settle

Lonely

Suddenly
a single bed
is much too small
the night's too long
bed-time silence roars
my feet are cold
my food is raw
the clock
goes slow
without You

Frank Rennie

Him 69

god is
Just
a Vision
a Circumstance
of fact
We're born
to live and
born to die
so Praise
the end
of that
Don't trouble
Me
with pious hopes
with Dreams
of Judgement
Day
for I'll Believe
the clergy
when they
Do
More
than they
Say

Frank Rennie

For My Mother

1. News Broken

You would think you wouldn't have noticed the small things
like the four cream-crackers: four squares with
four squares of orange cheese.
But small sights were never stronger and sounds too
in tones of voices offering cups of tea.

2. Shape

If it wasn't for that shape
my thoughts might never
have left the slab.

But where could I look,
ahead or within,
when the relief of a face
came through the shroud
and the body seemed
so down to earth.

3. Below the Window

She would take tea down here – no biscuit–
and just the quick glance at the magazine.
All this below the kitchen window;
always with a pan left on the boil.

Her tiger-lily failed
but the nasturtiums came
and the willow stake,
dead at each end,
grew out of hand.

4. Two Cemeteries

Red keal in a blur
on the blown fleeces.
The huddle crouches by
the easterly wall of Ui.
Its lichen yellows are in the lee.

I haven't patience for the clouds,
spectacular enough today
from Kebock Head to Arnish Point.
It's strange how eyes settle for detail
under this longstone lintel.
Trapped deer's heads, stone bones,
the bulge of flesh in a relief
of some Macleod lying in state.

Out the walls, into the westerly,
I want to be content with glimpses
of a sunny and stormblown fankle:
driftrope captured on a groyne
at the fatted limit of tide
but my mind is driving on the tar
that's laid out towards my town
and a burial ground in better repair.

Looking across Sandwick's draped urns
through the steel basket beacon
that stands on Sgeir Mhor and bears
to derricks breaking Glumaig's light,
I can't avoid a foreground stone
in marble we chose from a catalogue.
'A Devoted Wife And Mother'.

As gilt is sneaked upon my moss
I ask why she
had to live through us.

Ian Stephen

Limbo

In the sorry hours of the dogwatch
sitting to a faraway
Emmylou on the radio
singing about a boxer
I'm gazing through the doorway
at the sighing slack sea
restlessly taking its ease

D T Macdonald

Murchadh

A Mhurchaidh, the clouds
are scudding in fast.
It's a long walk to the meeting house
in the threat of rain.
Why bother tonight?
Your soul will last
another week. Perhaps.
But will your body hold out
until the last pictures of the psalm
drift out of sight
to meet the waves?

For peace of mind he
drags his body past
the Co-op and the schoolhouse.
The fear of pain
less than the fear of the might
of the Lord and His caste.
Another week. Perhaps.
But the years are too many on your frame
and the soaking you will take
will leave you nothing but
the Light of the Lord
and a small patch in the clay.

Siùsaidh NicNèill

Home Again

Home again
to the flat island
to see the horizontal washing
flapping manically
the sharp northeasterly
springing the pegs
from the line
and the smoke coughing
from the stack.
From the southwest
it would blow back
to choke the firesiders.

Siùsaidh NicNèill

A Tangible Memory

Your old blue jacket
still hangs behind the door.
Bobbles and fluff
and worn weaving
cling to the sleeves.
The cuffs sag sordidly
elastic long left by the fences.
And I saw you last
by the peats.
Your old blue jacket
hanging on the spade.

Siùsaidh NicNèill

No. 2 Pier

Leaning over
piers
tears spill
into the abysmal
grey seas
between us.

No choice
no fuss
just the
cost of
leaving

Lorraine Bruce

Reunion

She will set
her sail and
cast off this
fine ship
with its
billowing canvas
and the brasses
on fire in
the dying sun
she will come
and time will
be kind to you.

Lorraine Bruce

Bruce Kent boarding the *Suilven*

Ian Stephen

Woman Darning, Harris

Murdo Macleod

Carol-Anne, Shawbost 1992

Murdo Macleod

Dithis

Cha tig an aois leatha fhèin,
cha tig gu dearbha.
Bodach na shuidh' leis a' phàipear
a' bruidhinn air Montana
agus twins na caorach bhàine.

Cailleach a' brunndail rithe fhèin,
a' togail a sùilean
's a' coimhead ris a' ghleoc
a fhuair i ann a Yarmouth.

Bidh esan a' bruidhinn
air Cassius Clay,
air prìs na clòimh (dèan copan te),
air Winnipeg
far an robh i cho fuar
's gu robh anail nan each
reòthte
tighinn a-mach às am beul.

Bha pòsadh a' chlobha ann an taigh Iain Mhòir
agus phòs iad mi ri Dòmhnall Bàn
(feuch nach leig thu 'n teine bàs) –
Obh, obh, fuachd mo chnàmhan
's mi nach eil cho math 's a bha mi.

Air a' *Charmania*
bha iad a' tilgeadh
nan corp thar na cliathaich ...
corp Dan T cuideachd ...
ach chuir Doilidh stad orra ...

Bha mis' ann a Yarmouth ...
's bha sinn air an àirigh ...
na h-àirighean fad' às ...
Dh'fhalbh iad, na làithean ...
cha tig an t-àm sin air ais ...

Bodach is cailleach
nan suidh' 'n tac an teine
a' feitheamh ri cuireadh
gu saoghal mòr eile.

Alasdair Mac a' Ghobhainn

Lewis Thursday

The wind salt
flays flecked quartz
from angled gables.
Inside
a millionaire
wails Delta Blues
and politicians flicker
round questions tabled in response to news.

Rain
and dead grass
impress landscape on windows.
The surf crests phosphorescent
lighting gloom
and hatted widows, serene,
soar grace notes
round grave pillars in a bare-walled room.

Alasdair Smith

Clach an Truiseil

Your lichened length
first indicated certainty
to the unrecorded masters
of conjectured craft
then tonsured pilots
wondered as they steered past
heading towards solitude
by Polaris.

Sea-proved Northern symmetry
prowed Siorravig on your transit
and reluctant circumnavigators
windstrewn
brought infusions of Iberia.

Land-cleared cottars
scraping subsistence by six-oar
kept you on Muirneag's shoulder
and Sheep Isle * fishers
clawing leeshored off by canvas
embayed
outran the fleet of Bernera.

Now depth-routed tankships
lump the western circle
crustaceans
gather viviered * on Aisgeir's markings
clinkered pine
is compassed on your needle
but long-lined shark-mouthed white fish
no longer savour life in Shader.

Alasdair Smith

* *Sheep Isle is the Faroe Islands: in 1982 the Faroes fishing vessel* Borgin,
with machinery failure, grounded at Shader after trying
to outrun a storm with an auxiliary sailing rig.

* *Vivier tanks on creel-fishing vessels keep shellfish alive*
by circulating sea-water.

South

South
seventeen and ashore in Moravia
I'm soon dazed by the city
so I make for the shore
Atlantic surf
and live sand
straggled by a palm leaf tide wash.
My pinking skin
approximates the inner peeling
imperfect tanning
of imperial leather.
Glimpsed thatch in the distance
awakens affinity.

Alasdair Smith

Pool in Gaelic

for Jack Collom and Tom Peters

Paul the Australian sinks the eight
but the cue ball kicks back
into the corner pocket
and I keep the table
the local shark's up next
we flip for break, U.K. rules
I call heads – it's tails
strange customs
and the pockets are too small
but I don't care
it's Friday night in Dun Carloway
third pint of stout in hand
and a dozen Gaelic conversations
compete with the television
the local kid's eating my lunch
I shoot, miss again
sit down next to Seòras
oldtimer chasing rum with lager
"uh, Seòras
uh, dè am facal Gàidhlig, uh, 'pool'?"
"Och, no, there isn't one,
it's a modern thing"
almost dead, I run off four balls
then miss a tough bank shot
sit down and lose with honour
my pool game's not quite so bad
as my Gaelic tonight

John Wright

Rural Mailbox Project with sculptor Ian Brady at Achmore

Sam Maynard

Alastair Fraser putting the shot at the Barvas Show, Lewis   Sam Maynard

On the *Suilven*   Sam Maynard

Stalemate

These words I spoke
Never once shook far less broke
The bridge or barrier
Between us
Or even mildly threatened
Our peculiar and individual
Brand of silence
With the most tentative
Breach of the peace.

Squatting in this tense
Between offence and defence
Outwith your jurisdiction
Beyond my power
Princes in our tower
Deferring sentence
Desperate partners.

Roddy Murray

Puberty Prayer

Like a vessel of ripened blood
Under pressure
Ready for the burst
You prepare for dispersion
Among the other beings
To a place you won't hold
To a time you can't grasp

Morven Macdonald

Melancholy Song

The dress it hangs limp
The shoes are hen-toed
Make-up removed
My head feels up-turned
The music it ended
Me, I left with another drink
And some father's first son
Last night was so good
The drink was so sweet
Today I stand straight
Facing me in the mirror
My eyes too dark
To see into

Morven Macdonald

A' Chliath

on the lot's incline
a man labours
a frame pinned
with iron pegs

there
is the rod and
metre of his work

still the mercy moves
tender
beneath him
on this southern slope
on this spring day

William Macleod

Until Daybreak

the shadows
shoaling
above the lairs
and orchids
of Cladh Mhìcheil
are the fingerling,
soft-flanked
coal-fish
we make our
delicate soups
from

William Macleod

The Night of the Three Suppers

the netted salmon
flexes
like a sleeper
in the gaudy, perfect
sun

now that we
have tasted
him
we are wise
to that luxury

all night,
browsing like a
heavy-headed fish,
the rain
is avid
upon past lives

William Macleod

Dà Rathad

Carson a bu chòir dhomh gabhail
na slighe ceart, lom, fada?
Ged a tha an rathad air a bheil mi cam
agus tha na clachan a' gearradh mo chasan,
agus tha dìreadh an leothaid
gam fhàgail gun anail,
chan e an aon rud
a tha mise coimhead romham
latha an dèidh latha.
Agus shuas air an leathad
chì mi timcheall orm,
chì mi gu bheil barrachd ann dhòmhs'
na slighe cheart, fhada, lom.
Tha thusa cumail do shùilean air an aon rud
ceart, dìreach air do bheulaibh –
agus chan fhaic thu gu bheil an saoghal
ag atharrachadh timcheall ort.

Anna Frater

Two Roads

Why should I follow
the long, smooth, straight road?
Although the road I take is crooked
and the stones cut my feet,
and climbing the hill
leaves me breathless,
I am not confronted
by the same prospect
day after day.
And up on the hill
I can see around me,
I can see that there is more in store for me
than a straight, long, smooth road.
You keep your eyes fixed on one point
right in front of you –
and you cannot see
that the world is changing around you.

Anne Frater

An Teasach

A' crochadh bhon t-slabhraidh
tha 'n coire cur a sheanar às;*
agus na coirean a th' unnainn
a' goil leis an teasach a th' oirnn
airson ar sinnsearan
a spùtadh a-mach nan ceò.

An cridhe blàth a chaidh a ghluasadh
le gaol is cleas is ceòl
a' falbh air àile aotrom
gun fiù 's fead.

Ach èisdibh ri mo choire-sa
gus an cluinn sibh mo sgreuch
ma thòisicheas an teine
ri mo sheanair a thoirt asam.

Anna Frater

Eilean Phabail

Mar thusa, tha mise
nam dhà leth;
a' seòladh air cuan
ach ceangailte ri creagan m' àraich;
uaine agus flùran
a' sreap gu grian
agus nèamh;
creagan donn a' bàthadh
fo mhuir agus feamainn
agus dorchadas.

Faisg air daoine:
gan coimhead,
gan cluinntinn,
ach cha ruig iad orm –
tha mi ro fhad' air falbh.

Chan urrainn dhomh fàgail,
chan urrainn dhomh tilleadh,
's cha tig an dà leth ri chèile.

Anna Frater

Fever

Suspended from the hanging chain,
the fiercely boiling kettle
steams and we,
sweating in fevered haste,
reject our ancestry
in insubstantial vapour.

The heart that was moved
to love and play and music,
drifting away now on a fitful breeze,
without a departing whistle.

But if the fire
should overcome my heritage
my steam shall not
ascend without a screech.

Anne Frater

Bayble Island

Like you, I am
divided.
Floating on sea
but made fast
to my ground rock;
green and flowers
climbing to the sun
and heaven;
brown rocks drowning
under brine and tangle
in darkness.

Near people,
watching them,
hearing them,
but they cannot reach me –
distance is maintained.

I can't leave.
There's no way back.
Halves remain separate.

Anne Frater
(Translations by the poet)

155

Fiosrachadh

Ach an solas glas an latha seo
cuid a thuair fhaileis air d' ghnùis
is dh'fhaillich orm coimeasgadh an lìth –

air am faicinn sguabte le gaoith
anns na fiamha-craicinn fionnar
de bheanntan air astaran.

Niall Seadha

Rìghleachan

Rìghleachan geal fhaoileann
a' tuiteam air a' chaladh –
acras geamhraidh an lòineagan.

Niall Seadha
(Eadar-theangachadh le Niall Seadha agus a charaidean)

Insight

But in this day's grey light
some shadows' hues about your face
I have failed to blend in pigment –

are seen brushed with winds
in the cool skin tones
of miles-off hillsides.

Niall Shaw

Flurries

White flurries of seagulls
falling on the harbour –
winter-hungry flakes.

Niall Shaw

Comharra Stiùiridh

Siud an t-eilean às an t-sealladh
mar a shiùbhlas am bàta,
mar a chunnaic iomadh bàrd e
eadar liunn is iargan,
's fir eile a bha 'n teanga fo fiacaill,
's deòir a' dalladh –
dùbhradh neo-dhearbht is uinneagan a' fannadh.

Ach chan eil a' cheiste cho sìmplidh
don allmharach an comhair na bliadhna:
a-mach à tilleadh èiridh iargan
à roinn a chuir an saoghal an dìmeas.

Cuideachd, chan e siud m' eilean-s':
chaidh esan fodha o chionn fhada,
a' chuid mhòr dheth,
fo dheireas is ainneart;
's na chaidh fodha annam fhìn dheth,
'na ghrianan 's cnoc eighre,
tha e a' seòladh na mara anns am bì mi
'na phrìomh chomharr stiùiridh
cunnartach, do-sheachaint, gun fhaochadh.

Domhnall MacAmhlaigh

Landmark

There goes the island out of sight
as the boat sails on,
as seen by many a bard
through sorrow and beer
and by others, tongue under tooth,
and tears blinding –
and ill-defined shadow and windows fading.

But the matter is not so simple
to the one who's a yearly pilgrim:
out of returning sorrow rises
from a region the world has derided.

And, that is not my island:
it submerged long ago
the greater part of it
in neglect and tyranny –
and the part that submerged in me of it,
sun-bower and iceberg,
sails the ocean I travel,
a primary landmark
dangerous, essential, demanding.

Donald MacAulay
(Translation by the poet)

Notes on Poets

Michael Bartlett studied Celtic at Aberdeen University.
He taught in Italy and now teaches in Lewis, living in Brue. He is
the translator of the frontispiece poem by Dr Francesco Maria Di
Bernardo-Amato from the original Italian into both English and Gaelic.
Dr Bernardo-Amato is a Sicilian who now practices medicine near
Venice.

Murdo Morrison lived in Ballantrushal, a village north of Barvas on the
West side of Lewis. This translation, by the poet's nephew, Alasdair
Smith, and the editor, is indebted to the version quoted in *Devil in the
Wind* by Charles Macleod (Gordon Wright Publishing, 1979).

Murdo MacFarlane was born in Lewis and returned to live in
Melbost after a period in Canada. *Dàin Murchaidh* – lyrics with cassette
recordings – was published by An Comunn Gaidhealach in 1986.
This song was published in *An Toinneamh Dìomhair* (The Stornoway
Gazette, 1973).

Roderick MacLeod was from Stockinish, Harris. This song appears
in *An t-Eilean A Tuath*, edited by Dòmhnall Iain MacLeòid (Comunn
Leòdhais agus Na Hearadh, 1972). The translation is published for
the first time.

Sorley MacLean was born on Raasay. His Collected Poems are
published by Carcanet. *Somhairle* – an anthology celebrating his 80th
birthday – was published by Acair in 1991. Acknowledgement is made
to Carcanet Press.

Norman MacCaig was born in Edinburgh. His mother was from
Scalpay, Harris. Chatto and Windus published an updated Collected
Poems in 1991. Acknowledgement is made to Chatto and to *Chapman*
for this selection.

Roderick Macdonald is also a Church of Scotland minister, now retired.
He was born in North Uist and was minister of St Columba's, Stornoway
for many years. He has published two collections of his own poetry,
two books of Gaelic hymn translations and two of Burns translations,
including the complete works. This poem is from *Leth-cheud Bliadhna*
(Gairm, 1978).

Derick Thomson was Professor of Celtic at Glasgow University until his retirement in 1991. From the village of Bayble, he is a founder of *Gairm* magazine, Gairm Publications and the Gaelic Books Council. These poems are from *Creachadh na Clàrsaich* (Macdonald Publishers, 1982) and *Smeur an Dòchais*, (Canongate Press, 1991).

Iain Crichton Smith from Bayble, Lewis, writes poetry, novels, short-stories, drama and criticism in English and Gaelic. His Collected Poems was published by Carcanet in 1992. Acknowledgement is made to *Poetry Australia* where "Lewis" was published and to Carcanet, Gairm and Macdonald Publishers.

Colin N Mackenzie was born on the island of Taransay, off West Harris. He is a Church of Scotland minister and prolific author of short stories in books such as *Oirthir Tìm* (Gairm, 1969) and *Mar Sgeul a Dh'innseas Neach* (Glasgow University Celtic Department, 1971). His poems appear in *Gairm* and in *Baragab* (An Comunn Gaidhealach, Stornoway, 1991).

J Mesleard was born in France but has lived in Lewis since 1958. He worked as a teacher of French, served on Stornoway Lifeboat for 13 years and is now French Consular Agent for this area. The extract is from *In Memorium* (Outposts Publications).

Francis Thompson has lived in Stornoway for most of his life. He is the author of a large number of non-fiction books on Scottish subjects and of several collections of poetry published by Pulteney Press, Wick.

Sheila Macleod has lived in Lewis for most of her life but was born in New York. She had worked in journalism, broadcasting and drama. A novel in Gaelic is published by Acair.

Donald MacAulay is Professor of Celtic at Glasgow University. Born on Great Bernera, Lewis, he is the editor of *Nua-Bhàrdachd Ghàidhlig*, first published in 1976 and reprinted by Canongate several times since. His earlier poems were collected in *Seóbhrach ás a' Chlaich* (Gairm, 1967) He edited and contributed to *The Celtic Languages* (Cambridge University Press, 1992). *Chan Eil Ann Cho Seòlta ris an Fhoghar* appeared in *Gairm* and was translated for this book.

Norman Malcolm Macdonald was born in Canada and brought up in Lewis. He is the author of the novel *Calum Tod* (Club Leabhar and Canongate) and the Gaelic documentaries *Creach Mhór nam Fiadh*, *Call na h-Iolaire* and *Clann-Nighean an Sgadain*, and of many plays etc. in Gaelic and English. This extract from *Anna Campbell* is from the version performed at the Traverse Theatre. The English versions of these poems appeared in the Stornoway Gazette and *Chapman*.

Mairi Macdonald was born in Grimsay, North Uist, and has taught in Glasgow, Argyll and Skye. Her poems, published by Crois Eilein Publications, have appeared in *Chapman* and are included in *An Anthology of Scottish Women Poets* (Edinburgh University Press). Her short stories for young people, *Grima*, have been published by Acair.

Donald John Maciver was born and raised on Lewis. For many years a school-teacher, he is now Bilingual Policy Advisor to Comhairle nan Eilean. He has published a collection of short stories for adults, *Camhanaich* (Buidheann-foillseachaidh nan Eilean an Iar, 1982), and one for younger readers, *Grian is Uisge* (Gairm, 1991), as well as poetry in *Gairm*.

John Murray is from Barvas, Lewis. He has worked in Education and in Gaelic Broadcasting and is the author of numerous short stories, including the collection *An Aghaidh Choimheach* (Gairm, 1973 & 1993). His poetry has been published in *Gairm* and in *Somhairle* (Acair 1991).

Dolina Maclennan was born in Marivig, South Lochs and now lives in Perthshire. She has worked in theatre (7:84 Company) and in television (*Machair*). This poem appeared in *Scotia Rampant*.

Calum Graham, from Lewis, now lives in London. He is co-author with Duncan Gillies of *Thall 's A-Bhos*, a book of translations of classic short stories (Gairm, 1991). This poem first appeared in *Gairm*.

Tessa Ransford lives in Edinburgh and is Director of the Scottish Poetry Library. She is the author of several collections of poetry. Acknowledgement is made to Macdonald Publishers for permission to reprint this poem from *A Dancing Innocence*.

Ian Stephen was born in Stornoway in 1955 and is now a Coastguard Officer. He is the author of *Malin Hebrides Minches* (Dangaroo Press, Denmark 1983) and *Varying States of Grace* (Polygon, 1989). Acknowledgements to Polygon and to *Poetry Wales*.

Ian MacDonald is an Uibhisteach, but his mother is from Scalpay. He works for the Gaelic Books Council, which is based in Glasgow, and has had poems and stories published in *Gairm* and elsewhere.

Kenneth White is a Scot who works as an academic in France and has won numerous awards for his poetry, which is published in the UK by Mainstream, and by Penguin. Acknowledgement is made to Mainstream.

Aonghas MacNeacail is from Skye and is the author of three books of poetry in Gaelic, including *An Seachnadh agus Dàin Eile* (Macdonald Publishers, 1986). His most recent English work is *Rock and Water* (Polygon, 1990). This poem on Callanish was published as an illustrated card.

Anna Adams is the author of *Island Chapters* (Littlewood Press 1992) – prose and poetry describing her experience of the island of Scarp. Acknowledgement is made to Littlewood.

Myles Campbell grew up in Skye and has family background in Lewis. He is the author of three poetry collections: *Eileanan* (Glasgow University Celtic Department, 1980), *Bailtean* (Gairm, 1987) and *A' Càradh An Rathaid* (Coiscéim, Dublin, 1988). His work appears in several anthologies. Acknowledgement is made to Gairm for these poems from *Bailtean*.

Valerie Gillies is the author of several collections of poetry published by Canongate. She lives in Edinburgh and has made many visits to the Long Island. Acknowledgement is made to Canongate for this poem from *Bed of Stone* (Edinburgh 1984).

Angus Macmillan was born in Lemreway, Lewis. He is a member of the Lochies folk-group and now works in Dumfries as a psychologist.

Steve Moore was born in Reading and has lived in Scotland since 1987: Sutherland, Ayrshire, Harris and now Bayble, Lewis. He is also a composer.

Morag Henriksen grew up in Lochcarron and has family background in Harris. Head-teacher of Uig Primary School, Skye, her work has been broadcast and anthologised.

Donald Munro lives in South Argyll and has family background in Ness, Lewis. His poetry and prose has appeared in many periodicals and anthologies. Acknowledgement is made to *New Writing Scotland* and *Chapman*.

Tom Bryan was born in Canada and now lives near Ullapool. Editor of *Northwords*, he writes regularly for the West Highland Free Press. A collection of his poetry is due out from Chapman Editions.

Mary Montgomery was born in Aribhruaich and also has family background in Harris. She works for the Education Department of the BBC making Gaelic radio programmes for schools. She has taken part in the Irish-Scottish poetry exchange visits and has published one collection, *Eadar Mi 's a' Bhreug* (Coiscéim, 1988), while her work has also appeared in periodicals and anthologies. Acknowledgement is made to Coiscéim.

Janice Settle was born in Southward and now lives in Brenish. She holds a BA (Hons) in Textile Design and an MA. Her interests are Gaelic language, poetry and rock climbing.

Frank Rennie is originally from Tillicoultry, Clackmannanshire but now lives in the Ness area of Lewis. He is a self-employed consultant in rural development and a writer. *Him 69* was published in *Radical Scotland*, issue 16, 1985.

D T Macdonald was born in the Point district of Lewis. His jobs have included: labourer, Harris Tweed worker, shipping clerk, postman, Civil Servant and part-time lighthouse-keeper; the latter resulting in this poem.

Siùsaidh NicNèill lived recently in Skigersta, Ness before moving to Skye, where she works in Gaelic broadcasting and film.

Lorraine Bruce was born in Edinburgh and lived in Lewis for ten years. Presently working for Highland Printmakers, her poems have been accepted for *Harpies and Quines* and *Northwords*.

Alasdair Smith was born in Ballantrushall and now lives in Brue. Previously a Merchant Seaman, he is now a Coastguard Officer at Stornoway. His poems have been published by *Gairm*.

John Wright lives in Colorado, USA and has published three collections of poetry. This poem was written during a visit to the Long Island in 1992.

Roddy Murray is from Back and studied at Glasgow School of Art. He could be recognised as the front-man guitarist in *Local Hero* but is now Director of An Lanntair – the Stornoway-based Arts Centre.

Morven Macdonald was born and educated in Stornoway. She was the winner of a nationwide competition for young writers, organised by The Scotsman. She now lives in Edinburgh.

William Macleod is from Tolsta. He studied in Stirling University and in the United States. He now works for the BBC, in Glasgow. Acknowledgement is made to *Prism*, Canada.

Anne Frater was born in Stornoway and educated at Bayble School, the Nicolson Institute and Glasgow University. Her poems in Gaelic have been published in many periodicals and anthologies. Acknowledgement is made to *Gairm* and Polygon.

Niall Shaw was educated at the Nicolson Institute and lives in Back, Lewis. He works for the Lewis Council of Social Service and does freelance typesetting and graphic design. He has contributed to the design of this book.

Notes on Photographers

Bill Lucas has lived in Stornoway for many years, operating the freelance 'Hebridean Press Agency'. He is a regular contributor to the Press and Journal.

Iain Macleod was raised in Ness and Stornoway. He is Fisheries Development Office for Comhairle nan Eilean. He was the winner of the first open photography competition originated by An Lanntair.

John Mackinnon is from Harris. He has worked as Staff Photographer for the Stornoway Gazette and now works in stills and video photography for Eòlas.

John Maclean lives in Coll, Lewis. He is a self-taught photographer. The Stornoway Girl portrait was taken in Inaclete Road in 1990. His portrait of Kenneth Campbell was taken in the subject's home in 1987 and was the winner of a nationwide competition.

John Charity has lived in the Ullapool area for many years and works as a freelance photographer. His work has been widely published and exhibited. Recent examples include the cover of James Miller's *A Fine White Stoor* (Balnain Books, 1992).

Becka Dilworth was brought up in Harris and was educated in Sir E Scott School, Tarbert and the Nicolson Institute. She is a recent graduate of Napier University. Her photographs were used to illustrate the catalogue for a Steve Dilworth exhibition in 1992.

Jeremy Sutton-Hibbert, born in Glasgow in 1969, was awarded the Ian Parry Memorial Award and Felix Mann Memorial Award for his photographs of Romania. His work appears in many UK national newspapers and is published regularly in Scotland On Sunday.

Sam Maynard lives in Stornoway and is proprietor of the Eòlas agency, working in stills, video and film. His work has been exhibited in the Third Eye Centre and at An Lanntair and published in *Malin Hebrides Minches, As an Fhearann, Somhairle*.

Ian Stephen has exhibited photographs in several North of Scotland galleries and published them in publications including The Scotsman and Scotland on Sunday.

Barbara Ziehm moved from Hamburg to Stornoway in 1983. This photograph was part of a project to express the need for improved playground provision and was published in the West Highland Free Press.

Murdo Macleod is from Shawbost, Lewis and now lives in Edinburgh. His freelance press photography is widely published and his work is included in many publications including *As an Fhearann* (An Lanntair), *An Aghaidh na Siorraidheachd/In the Face of Eternity* (Polygon) and *Somhairle* (Acair). An exhibition stemming from his Edinburgh project on the homeless of Edinburgh was An Lanntair's opening exhibition.